AF541770

DPH SPORTS SERIES

GYMNASTICS

H. C. Dubey

DISCOVERY PUBLISHING HOUSE
New Delhi-110002

First Published 199
Reprint 2006

ISBN 81-7141-472-9

© Author

Published by:
DISCOVERY PUBLISHING HOUSE
4831/24, Ansari Road, Prahlad Street,
Daryaganj, New Delhi-110 002 (*INDIA*)
Phone: 3279245
Fax: 91-11-3253475

Printed at:
Amit Enterprises Delhi

PREFACE

The need of having a sports series felt because today's situation of the world is not conducive to peace, all round there is destruction, despair, conflict and war; war if not between two nations then within the country itself. In a world where there are some 820 million people unemployed or under-employed, and where 86 million people are born every year, it is not surprising that one out of every four individuals lives in absolute poverty. The *Discovery Publishing House* by Publishing this series seeks to get positive response as—to means by which sports can promote and propagate peace and international cooperation. Sportsmen form a large identifiable cadre. We visualises a situation where a conscious efforts is made all over the world to train the sportspersons to spread the message of peace and international cooperation. Instead of peace keeping efforts through arms and army, the sportspersons may be used as soldiers of peace in a subtle manner. The effort is to make the realize the contribution of sports as a factor for sustainable development, peace keeping and international cooperation.

In developing countries, sports development cooperation is still in the need of justification and steadfast arguments. Many people ask the question "why invest in sports in developing countries for which water supply, health service and agriculture projects are much better suited? An apt reply to this question may be "for many of the people of a developing country,

Sports is the only 'Sweaty' Leisure-time activity. Sports represents a moment of joy in the midst of hard poverty-stricken and dirty everyday life. Doing sports even makes one's work go more smoothly the next day.

This series will be useful to the sports promoters, organisers, coaches and other persons related or interested in sports.

Editor

CONTENTS

1 INTRODUCTION

The sport of gymnastics encompasses a vast field of activity. It includes not only the ten Olympic events (floor exercise, long horse vault, rings, horizontal bat', parallel bars, and side horse for men and floor exercise, cross horse vault, beam, and uneven bars for women) but also such varied activities as trampolining, tumbling, flying rings, rope climbing, dual balancing, and pyramid building.

The discussion of each of these includes (1) a consideration of the basic concepts underlying the techniques used in the event, and (2) a series of brief analyses of selected techniques to show how these concepts apply in specific cases. With respect to the latter, elementary techniques are given preference over more advanced ones, although (where possible) these too receive some attention.

Floor exercise

The gymnastic movements used in floor exercises are widely regarded as forming the foundation upon which the rest of gymnastics is built. For this reason, the basic concepts underlying these movements deserve careful consideration. Floor exercises are generally composed of leaps; springing and tumbling movements (including necksprings, headsprings, rolls, cartwheels, somersaults, etc.); and held positions exhibiting balance, suppleness, and strength.

In leaps (and in those springing and tumbling movements in which the gymnast is projected into the air) success depends on the ability:

1. to acquire lift and rotation at takeoff,
2. to control rotation while in the air,
3. to control both translation and rotation on landing, and
4. to do these three things in an aesthetically pleasing way.

The flight path of a gymnast who has left the ground (like that of all other projectiles) is determined by the velocity and height of the center of gravity at the instant of takeoff. Thus any attempt to improve the gymnast's performance by acquiring more lift must involve modifying either or both of these quantities if it is to have the desired effect. The rotation that a gymnast acquires at takeoff derives from one or both of two sources--a couple and/or an eccentric force.

Once the gymnast has left the ground, the only way in which he (or she) can control rotation is by adjusting the moment of inertia of the body. By bringing the masses of the various body parts closer to the axis of rotation through the, enter of gravity, the gymnast can increase the angular velocity of the body; conversely, by moving them farther away, the gymnast can decrease the angular velocity (conservation of angular momentum). The extent to which the gymnast can make such adjustments is generally limited, however, by the nature of the aesthetic and technical requirements of the activity. For example, a gymnast could tuck toward the end of a neckspring and thereby increase angular velocity. There is no doubt, though, that such a manoeuvre would be much less aesthetically pleasing than one in which the body was kept fully extended throughout the flight. Furthermore, it fails to meet the technical demands of the movement, which require that such springs be completed in an essentially straight position. Under such circumstances it should be clear that while the gymnast can exert a small measure of control over the rotation when in the air, the most important determining factor as far as rotation is concerned is not what is done in the air but what is done on the ground during the takeoff. For it is here that is decided what angular momentum the gymnast will have during the flight and how long this angular momentum will have to take its effect (that is, how long the gymnast will be in the air).

At the instant the gymnast lands, the gymnast's body is rotating about an axis through its center of gravity, which is itself translating. If the gymnast wishes to come to a stop (rather than to move off immediately into another movement), he (or she) must evoke such forces from the landing surface as will cancel this translation and rotation. The logical (and most used) method of doing this is for the gymnast to land so that the reaction forces evoked act eccentrically. These eccentric forces provide a rotating effect of such magnitude and direction as to reduce the angular velocity to zero. Their translatory effect similarly reduces the linear motion of the center of gravity to zero. If the gymnast wishes to move straight into another stunt, he (or she) tries to evoke a reaction consistent with the needs of this stunt. If these include a continuing rotation in the same direction (as in. say, a flipflop followed by a back somersault), the gymnast endeavors to obtain a reaction that rather than canceling the rotation at least permits some of it to be retained, and perhaps even enhances it. On the other hand, if the gymnast wants to follow with a movement involving a rotation in the opposite direction (and this, it might be said, is much less likely), he (or she) tries to more than cancel the existing rotation and thus acquire some angular momentum in the desired direction. Another important factor concerning landing is the distance over which the body moves while being brought to rest or while having its motion redirected. The basic concepts involved in rolling movements (forward and backward rolls, cartwheels, etc.) are exactly the same as those described above in connection with the springs and the other tumbling movements, except that here the gymnast does not leave the ground and is therefore not concerned with those factors that create lift.

For held or static positions the gymnast endeavors to assume as stable an equilibrium position as is possible and consistent with aesthetic and technical demands. The gymnast thus seeks to have:

1. the gravity line passing through the midpoint of the base--or, to express it another way, to have the distance from the gravity line to the limits of the base as large as possible.
2. the center of gravity as low as possible.

Movement observation

Movement is transient and in the teaching situation is rarely recorded by notation, by still or cinephotography or by video-taping, although the latter does offer exciting possibilities as a teaching and learning aid when it is available. However, one way in which teachers and children can widen their knowledge of movement is by trying to see and to understand what is happening while it is happening. This is movement observation, the degree or depth of which will vary with the circumstances. Observation could be defined as seeing with understanding since in observing there is an active seeing of movement involving sympathetic participation by the observer rather than watching passively, or merely looking.

It is vital for a teacher to observe children, whatever the subject or situation. It is through observation that the successful teacher assesses the moods, attributes, needs and potential of individuals and groups. The observation of children moving should not be confined to the gymnastics lesson. Observing children at play, as they move around the school, in the classroom, as well as during other physical education activities, can be most valuable. In such situations the experienced observer can learn much about the children he is teaching through an understanding of their movement behaviour. The junior or Middle school teacher has a unique opportunity to know his pupils since he is with them in most of their activities. In the selecting of gymnastic material this knowledge could help him to widen their movement experience and cater for their movement needs. Similarly, what the junior or Middle school teacher observes in the gymnastic lesson should be of value in the classroom, contributing to a better understanding of each child.

The physical education specialist whether in a Middle or Secondary school has the opportunity to become an expert observer of movement. However, he must realise that he is seeing children in one situation only, revealing though that situation undoubtedly is.

In the teaching of gymnastics it is particularly important that the teacher should observe well. Within a lesson the movement experience is guided by a series of tasks, each dependent upon the reaction to the preceding challenge. This demands acute observation. The difficulty arises sometimes when there are many answers to a given challenge and often the teacher will have as many different solutions offered as there are children in the class. Moreover, there are few set responses and usually the work is exploratory. Unless the teacher is able to observe adequately it is unlikely that either he or his class will gain satisfaction from working in this manner, because of his inability to select, use and develop what he sees.

The ways in which a teacher observes his class *generally* are obvious, for example, young children coming from a crowded classroom to the relative freedom of the hall or playground may immediately show a desire to exploit the space. Seeing this the teacher might give action tasks, such as running and jumping, before expecting more controlled work as in balancing. Prior to the gymnastic lesson an older class may have had a period where concentrated mental effort has been. demanded. When the children are beginning to warm up their actions may appear lethargic and through a quick assessment of their mood the teacher may decide to devote time to a guided enlivening of the body.

At the same time the teacher is also concerned with more *specific* and immediate problems to which observation can provide the answer. When a task is set it is vital to see from the response if the movement ideas involved have been understood and are being used profitably. As a result of his observation the teacher may need to clarify the task for the whole class, or it may be that individuals require further help.

Sometimes the teacher may be looking for those whose response to a challenge is worth showing to the rest of the class. The way in which children can be helped to observe is dealt with later, but here the connection between observation teacher, selecting and "showing" is seen. In his selection the teacher is often setting a standard of work, re he should choose children whose work contains something of value. Demonstration in its narrowest sense is not normally relevant to this way of teaching gymnastics. However, it is often expedient to select children to show their work to the rest of the class. It may be that several children are chosen because

(a) they have variety, or

(b) they have a particular point in common.

For example, perhaps two or three will choose to balance on hands, but each arranges the rest of his body differently and the teacher may wish to point out such possibilities to the rest of the class. Selection by the teacher necessitates quick observation and this must be trained consistently. The poor observer may find himself faced with exciting activity from which he is unable to extract anything of significance. A pitfall to be avoided is that of looking only at those individuals who can be expected to find a worthwhile solution. If the same children show their work lesson after lesson, while the less spectacular or less able individuals are precluded, then the opportunity of the latter making a valuable contribution is lost. The skilled observer should be able to watch and select from the whole class.

Although of necessity much of the observation is concerned with the class or groups, opportunities should be to observe individuals. Through observation over a of time the teacher can build up a valuable "movement of each child. He can learn to recognise and help not only the skilled and the able but also the apparently foolhardy, the accident-prone, the nervous and lacking confidence. To the beginner it may appear as if this method of teaching is only for the expert observer of movement, but this is not so. All teachers are continuously adapting and, adjusting their teaching material to the needs and reactions' of their classes and observation is one way of gaining feedback. However, it is stressed that to be successful in this work it is essential to observe movement consciously and to set out to train this faculty deliberately.

In the teaching of gymnastics the understanding of movement and movement observation are complementary; each will gain from the other. When beginning to observe the teacher may see only those aspects of movement to which he himself is sympathetic and stresses in his own work. However, just as the successful teacher avoids imposing his own movement preferences on his class, so the sympathetic observer must train himself to look for all aspects of gymnastics and not be confined by his own movement experiences. The following is suggested as a framework upon which the teacher can build his observation of class and individual. Although it is hoped that teachers will endeavour to observe children moving in many situations, it is recognised that most observation of necessity takes place during a lesson. The headings are basic, being valid for both general and specific observation. The examples given are from typical gymnastic situations that a teacher might observe.

In the observation of gymnastics the teacher's attention is upon four separate but related aspects within the context of the theme being taught.

1. Body—The observer determines what the body i doing by looking at part, parts and the whole.
2. Space—The observer sees *where the* body is moving noting levels, directions and pathways.
3. *Speed, Tension and Energy—The observer* considers bow the body is moving by assessing the speed, tension and the energy expended.
4. *Relationships*—The observer notes the relation between the body and the floor,", apparatus, partner and group.

Body

In gymnastics many different actions can be distinguished. Some of these involve the body as a whole, while in others a part or parts are more important than the rest. It is the interplay and relation of parts to each other and to the whole body that concerns the observer. Curling, stretching, twisting and jumping are examples of actions normally involving the whole body. Through observation the teacher determines if this is so or if parts are omitted from the action. In curling, for example, the head and parts of the spine are often neglected. When stretching, children find difficulty in feeling this action through to their extremities and so what is happening to the hands, head and feet needs to be observed. In flight children often anticipate the landing through lack of confidence and this results in the upper half of the body inhibiting the flight, for instead of carrying on the upward thrust of the legs, the stress is downward, the focus being towards the landing area. The teacher who observes these "bodily happenings" can then help his class to be more aware of what the body is doing and this should lead to more sensitive work.

In many actions, although the whole body is alive to the movement taking place, some parts because of their function have more emphasis than others as when sliding on the trunk occurs. The part of the body in contact with the ground is held in position, while one or more of the limbs provides propulsion by vigorous pushing or pulling. In such situations the limbs carry the main stress of the action. When a balance is held and then the weight transferred, the part that is to bear the weight assumes importance as it is prepared and placed in position.

In observing what the body is doing the teacher can see the extent to which the class needs further help. Similarly the next step in teaching can be determined. If the task "experiment with balancing the body on asymmetric or uneven bases" is given then in this challenge what the body is doing is being stressed and the teacher would find his teaching points by observation based on the following questions.

(a) Are all the ways of producing an uneven base being used—i.e. two unlike parts from different sides, or two parts from the same side, or two like parts placed unevenly?

(b) Are individuals challenging themselves to the fun, trying difficult inverted balances?

(c) Are the balances being held or moved through?

(d) Is there an awareness of what the rest of the body is doing above the base?

Whenever the challenges are specific to the body or action tasks are given, the teacher should always observe the body first, for this ensures that the teaching point is pursued and developed. Often there is a temptation to deviate. An inexperienced teacher might follow the initial task with the suggestions that the class "add variations of speed". This shows not only lack of movement understanding but also poor observation. Progressions are based on the response to each challenge and it is unlikely that a class concerned with experimental balances will indicate a need to consider speed changes as well.

When observing the body, in addition to looking for the interplay between the parts and the whole, as in climbing a rope, the teacher must take other considerations into account. Sometimes the lower half is more important than the upper, as in taking off from the ground. Often one side is stressed more than the other, as in the beginning of a cartwheel. The movement possibilities of the body are virtually limitless and persistent observation is required to recognise what is happening and then to act upon what is seen.

Space

The need to observe the body in space during floorwork depends upon the task set. The spatial aspect may be of primary or secondary importance. In an introductory task of "alternately travel high in the air and low along the ground" the first observation would be directed towards the use of level. It would be necessary to see if the high and low levels were being exploited or if the movement was taking place in a meagre extension of the medium level. In another introductory task of "travel on different body parts" it would be essential to ensure that this was happening before observing the use of directions. Levels, directions, pathways and body shape are often incidental to the main action of the body during floor work. Just as observation should not be directed immediately towards these aspects, so the class should not consider them until clarity and understanding of what the body is doing are shown.

When a spatial theme is taught there is much to observe. In the task of "travel, using different directions" the observant teacher may see many variations. Some children will remain on an habitual pathway, such as circling the hall or gymnasium, and while on this track will travel forwards backwards or sideways. Others will concentrate on a varying track composed of lines, zig-zags, loops and curves which changes their front in relation to the space, but retain one direction, usually forwards. Having realised this the teacher might reword his challenge or decide to bring the different responses to the attention of the children by selecting several for them to observe.

Apparatus is often arranged so that each

individual can select his own actions and pathways and here the teacher can observe if these are well correlated. One child might always approach each piece along a straight pathway, another only change direction on the floor between apparatus and in both cases limited use of path and track would probably narrow the choice of action. A third child might adjust and shift about on apparatus in order to change direction because of an inappropriate arrival. If a teacher can observe such situations and understand the resulting difficulties he should be in a better position to offer constructive help.

Speed, tension and energy

Although what the body is doing is often of prime importance, how the body acts is also a vital consideration. When the speed of an action is assessed it is not sufficient to decide if the rate is quick or slow, although this is a beginning. Phases where acceleration or deceleration occur, as well as the rhythm and climax in a sequence, must be noted. A child may not get on to a high box because he has failed to build up his speed during his approach. Another child may be unable to hold a balance on a bar because he has not, appreciated the need to decelerate into the balance. Actions such as jumping for a rope, helping a partner to achieve flight, landing on a narrow surface from a swing on a rope are often inefficient because the timing is poor. A tea who can appreciate when lack of timing defeats the aim of a action will have taken the first step towards being able to give positive help to his class.

Many children fail to get over high apparatus with weight on hands. This is because they cannot produce a strong energetic action in the upper part of the body or they do not realise that any change in tension is required. A teacher who by observation can pinpoint the reasons for inefficient and unsuccessful actions is more likely to help the performers than one whose comments remain at the "try harder", "get over next time" level.

Sometimes the speed, tension and energy may appear secondary to what the body is doing. When attempting to roll for the first time, young children can be helped if attention is drawn to the action of the body rather than the tension and energy required. On acquiring the skill, however, it may be of great importance to stress these, particularly when the roll is one of a series or part of a sequence. In many actions there is an equal stress on what the body is doing and how it performs the action. The takeoff to achieve flight from the ground is a typical example. The action of the body is from flexion into extension but unless this is done quickly and with considerable energy no flight results. Similarly, the flight phase itself can be impaired by too little or too much tension. In observing ineffective takeoffs and flight the teacher must see which of these vital ingredients is missing or over-stressed and help accordingly.

Relationships

In gymnastics the body can never be considered who isolation. Whatever the action there is always a relation between the body and the ground or apparatus or people. This relation, whether it results in contact or not often taken for granted. A class showing little sensitivity,., in this respect usually reflects a teacher who has failed to observe well and consequently has done nothing to remedy the deficiency. In getting on to a small box from the floor with weight on hands a young child may not appreciate the importance of where he places his hands. He may put them too near the edge, so that there is little room for the rest of his body, or too far away, so that he is unable to take weight on them. Having observed this the teacher could suggest that he climbs on to the box and finds out where to place hands and feet in relation to each other and to his intended action.

An older child trying to swing from a rope to land on a box top some distance away will often continue to push the box from him not realising what is the cause. The teacher who has observed that the approach is from the side instead of from above the box, or that the body is rigid instead of waving up" over the feet on contact, is likely to help the child to be successful.

Another child attempting to roll along the top of a box might do this as if on a mat and consequently roll off the end. The teacher who observes that this child is unaware of the relation between the length of his back, the size of his roll and the space available may well be able to give constructive help.

In many activities which involve flight on, off and over apparatus, the placing of the hands determines what the rest of the body can do. When helping an individual in this situation, the teacher should observe where the hands are placed on the apparatus and how the rest of the body is used in relation to the hands, as this often indicates the reason for an unsuccessful attempt. It is mentioned in the chapters devoted to partner and group work that such situations should not be explored until the teacher considers the class capable of benefiting from them. The decisions to start such work will be based on knowledge of the class which has been built up by constant observation. Once working with others is taking place the teacher needs to be particularly alert to see that this is progressing in a safe and profitable way. Concern for the Partner or group has to be encouraged and fostered by the teacher.

When observing a small group trying out ways and lowering each other the teacher needs to be alert to the amount of give and take that is necessary. He will see those who readily adapt to being one of a group and those who find this difficult. From his knowledge of the individuals concerned the teacher should know the best way to deal with the situations observed.

When a selected challenge is presented to his class the teacher will normally know which aspect to observe first whether "what" the body is doing is more important than "how" it is acting, and what to look for subsequently However, it is often necessary to consider the movement as a whole to determine its main characteristics. This happens when a teacher finds that a child has decided what he wants to do in answer to a movement challenge but for some reason is unable to carry out his intention. If the teacher is to help within the context of the situation he must observe what the child is trying to do and how he is setting about it, or, if this is not clear, ask for a verbal explanation.

The teacher must decide from his observation and knowledge of movement what are the essential characteristics of the action or series of actions, the inherent factors that make it what it is. For example, in jumping the body is always thrust into the air and although the jumps may vary in size the thrust is always present to a greater or lesser degree. Once these are determined they must be seen in relation to the child and how his attempt differs from that which will bring success. When these movement discrepancies have been discovered the teacher is in a position to give positive, help.

In addition there are certain biomechanical factors which h' determine to a large extent what the body can and cannot do in, for example, flight and balance. If a teacher's observation is supplemented by such knowledge, which becomes increasing relevance as advanced work is reached, teaching should be enhanced.

It is through an understanding of movement, a knowledge of each child and observation that a teacher should relate the movement essentials of actions with the a movement characteristics of the individual.

Observation by the class

Just as observation is vital to the teacher so children can be trained to observe and helped to profit from what they see. The visual is important as a way of learning and can help to widen an individual's movement vocabulary. Points which would otherwise remain obscure might be clarified by watching classmates tackling a common problem. It is in seeing the variety of ways in which a challenge can be met that the scope of a movement theme is appreciated. This is particularly so when observation is followed immediately by the children exploring ideas for themselves.

Beginners usually try to copy the actions seen but later children can select from the movement ideas observed and make them their own by modification and adjustment. The movement imagination is usually stimulated and enlivened by observation.

Through observation children begin to appreciate their own movement characteristics in relation to those of others. The child who naturally moves quickly can, by observation, recognise slow, unhurried movement and with the teacher's help this can be developed into an awareness of moving slowly when work is resumed. The ability to perceive one's own movement preferences as well as limitations can be vital in the establishing of a self-concept.

When beginning observation with a class the teacher has the possibilities of:

(a) selecting two or three individuals whose work is worth showing to the rest of the class,

(b) dividing the class in half so that each group in turn observes and moves, or

(c) dividing the class into couples so that each child observes his partner in turn.

In (a) the observation is focussed but the children showing may be self-conscious. In *(b)* the observation is more dispersed but those moving are unlikely to be inhibited and each child experiences both situations. In each method the teacher has two groups both of which need guidance in order to benefit from the experience.

The observers should be given one point to look for first, e.g:

"What parts of the body take weight?"

"Is there an increase or decrease in speed?"

"Which direction is being stressed?"

As skill in observing increases more than one movement, aspect can be considered, *e.g.*:

"What is the essential difference between these sequences? "

"What have these people in common?"

"What varying relationships occur in this group sequence?"

After observation the children should be able to make a brief', analysis of what they have seen and offer constructive criticism.

The performers may need to be told beforehand that their work is to be seen. This ensures that they are prepared both mentally and physically. Some children obviously enjoy being selected and this often provides motivation for further effort. Others lack confidence but the teacher can do much to create an atmosphere of mutual help so that this difficulty is eventually overcome. Having shown his work the mover should receive helpful comments. Occasionally sequences may be selected that only partially fulfil a challenge and this situation must be handled carefully by the teacher. It can be successful only when the relationships are such that the performers have confidence in the sympathy and understanding of the teacher and the rest of the class. Then an exchange of ideas and views can be valuable and do much to add to an understanding of the movement problems involved.

The third method, (c), has advantages in that the observation is directed towards one person and the performer is unlikely to be self-conscious. It is essential in this situation that the teacher gives specific observation points. The disadvantages are that some of the work seen may not particularly good and the teacher cannot easily check that the couples have profited by the experience.

After observation it is usual for the class to work again the same task. The children who observed must be given a chance to put what they have seen and learnt into practice Those who performed will have been given help which they can now implement. When the whole class resumes work it is an excellent opportunity for the teacher to see if the time spent on observation has been worthwhile.

The teacher should be able to use class observation appropriately. In starting a new gymnastic theme observation is of little value when the work is at the early exploratory stage. Too much observation too soon can be limiting. In partner and group work observation usually occurs during the working out of ideas and this not only enables movements to be matched where applicable but also fosters sympathetic work.

Observation is one way in which appreciation of logical movement can be gained. Younger children are invariably able to see this first in the work of others before they can make a similar assessment of their own efforts while older children are able to appreciate the varied work of others of differing abilities. Through observation children are given the opportunity not only of watching others but also of adding to their own movement understanding. Furthermore, when children observe perfected gymnastic work it is a situation in which the teacher can guide and aid their critical faculties by pointing out those features and attributes of the performance that might be termed aesthetic.

The place of observation in any one lesson needs careful consideration. Abused it can kill the pace of a lesson, used skilfully it enhances both movement and understanding. Young children and beginners do not need to observe often but older children can profit by short intensive sessions. The experienced teacher will probably include observation by the class of floor or apparatus work or both in most lessons. It is through an understanding of the value of this way of working and seeing it in relation to teaching gymnastics generally that a teacher is most likely to use observation profitably.

2
ELEMENTARY BODY MANAGEMENT

The ability to control and manage the body would appear as one of the main essentials in any given movement situation. In gymnastics this is certainly a prior consideration. Children must first be guided towards an awareness of the capabilities of the body. Later they can be helped to acquire greater mastery, in terms of control and management, which in turn leads to heightened enjoyment and satisfaction that springs from increased skill. Unlike learning a foreign language, gymnastic movement is not new to the beginner; children, however young, will have already gained a degree of bodily skill, and will certainly have experienced joy and satisfaction in moving. Once the child is placed in the learning situation, however, although use is made of movements he has already mastered, the emphasis now is on a growing consciousness of what the body is doing, of how it is moving, and where it is going. Once this awareness has been fostered, the children's habitual movements are extended to include new skills, which when mastered, become part of a wider, more varied movement vocabulary.

The term "body awareness" has over the years become for many something of a meaningless catchphrase; in this text, however, it denotes the individual's experiential identification of himself in terms of his body concept within the gymnastic environment. In everyday life it is essential that each individual evolves a basic vocabulary of habit actions such a." walking, sitting, eating and dressing. Although the kinesthetic sense has been involved in the acquisition of these skills, conscious effort in performing them lessens until, eventually they become habitual and a conscious awareness of what is happening is no longer required. In civilised communities, interest in and awareness of movement are on the whole subdued; movements tend to be restricted and restrained, children's actions become inhibited and retarded through contact with a variety of adverse situations. It is this awareness of what the body is doing, how one part moving affects the whole, and the relation and interplay of body parts in action, which must be stimulated if the movement vocabulary and ability of individuals is to become enriched and vital.

The following elementary themes of Locomotion, Stillness, Weight Bearing and Transference of Weight all involve guiding children towards an awareness of the body in action. Although there is variety within this selection certain correlations exist but for clarification each aspect is cod in isolation. It should be noted that these are dealt with in a form of progression so that each new idea utilises the knowledge and skill acquired in previous work. Locomotion, that is travelling, is achieved by the transference of weight from one part of the body either to the same part, or to another in succession. This is normally brought about by weight being tra.sferred on to one or both feet as in stepping, running, hopping or skipping, but in gymnastics this is by no means the only method. Ground can be covered by hands supporting the weight of the body while feet overtake or follow, as in cartwheels and crouch jumps. Another way of travelling is where contact with the floor is maintained and the body kept curled and compact as in rolling. This can be experienced on a variety of body Surfaces and in any direction. When the body is ejected into the air and flight takes place the body travels through space, and although this too is usually achieved from feet to feet, other parts can be used to eject and receive body weight. The body can also be moved from one place to another in a sliding action, which usually involves large surfaces such as front, back or hips. In this instance, although travelling results, the body itself may or may not move, for after the initial impetus the shape can change or the position be maintained whilst sliding takes place.

This aspect of gymnastics is a relatively simple idea an when the basic methods of travelling over the floor have bee explored and understood, cannot profitably be sustained for any length of time without recourse to more demanding situations. Extensions can be made to the original notion through the use of apparatus which greatly increases the range of practical possibilities or the focus of attention c be redirected towards the more cognitively demanding themes of weight bearing and transference of weight..

Teaching

Although locomotion is a fundamental aspect of

gymnastics, in the early stages of introducing this work to children, it is dealt with in a very elementary way. It is, however, useful starting point, as most young children are interested in ways of getting from one place to another, and are concerned with the "going" and with the parts of the body used when covering ground.

It is sufficient at this stage to experiment in order to discover the various possibilities of travelling, and experience should be given in the number of ways in which feet or hands and feet are used in conjunction. Children should be encouraged to use the trunk as well as parts of the limbs on which to progress and resulting actions should include such activities as crawling, sliding, running, hopping, leaping, rolling and rocking.

Young children are often unable to change readily from one action to another and therefore transitions are rarely achieved fluently. Nevertheless most children between the, ages of six and nine enjoy repeating the same action sever times and can be encouraged to do this. In some cases rhythm will be established in repetition which children fin most exciting and satisfying. Action phrases including various ways of travelling can be introduced at this stage where simple transitions only are involved and weight bearing, is restricted to a limited number of body parts. These can be related to the movement preferences of children of approximately this age, for example, most will choose to run, jump land and slide to a stop; or run, jump and turn in the air, land and roll; whilst to run, dive and slide would be characteristic action sequence for many.

A later development for older children is to

combine travelling actions, where they learn to move easily and with agility throughout a sequence, with a, number of body parts talking weight in turn.

Apparatus

The elementary aspect of locomotion will mainly concern Primary teachers; however the specialist teaching in the Middle, school or first year Secondary pupils may be tackling the same theme, but will probably have a greater variety of apparatus with which to work. Suggestions for work on apparatus are, therefore, dealt with separately for Primary classes, although the principles of providing apparatus for work on locomotion remain the same for any age group.

Opportunities should be given for travelling with specific body parts suggested-

1. on the feet,
2. using hands and feet,
3. on hands only.

or the stress can be on bodily actions

4. by sliding,
5. by rolling,
6. by gripping and releasing alternately.

Locomotion on the feet

Obstacles should be provided to jump over, to get in an out of, or on and off, along, or to go from side to side.

Primary—Apparatus such as canes or hoops supported on" skittles, individual mats, ropes and jumping stands, planks,, chairs, low tables and steps all provide suitable challenges' for this activity.

Middle and secondary— Forms used both narrow and broadside uppermost and slightly inclined, mats and mattresses, will initially give sufficient opportunity for experimentation with the basic idea of travelling using feet only.

Locomotion using hands and feet

Classes can be introduced to the idea that hands can lead while feet follow, that hands can lead and feet overtake, that hands and feet can be on the same or on different levels, and that limbs can work together or alternately.

Primary—Ladders or planks used horizontally or inclined on stools or climbing frames, ropes or nets where the children can clamber, scramble and climb, would be sufficient to stimulate a variety of ways of travelling using hands and feet.

Middle and Secondary— Forms used as suggested in 1. above, bars or any type of hinged wallbars, ropes or wooden climbing ladders, planks or box tops should present beginners with a sufficient variety of experimental situations.

Locomotion on hands only

As it is impossible for the majority of children to travel on the floor taking weight on hands alone, this possibility can be more thoroughly explored on apparatus. There are two essential differences between using the hands on the floor and on apparatus. One is that on apparatus the hands are able to grip, an action impossible on a flat surface. Secondly, whereas on the floor the body must be above the hands if these are to support the weight, on apparatus it may be suspended below the weight bearing part, an entirely different experience. Also if inversion is involved, as it will be in most cases, the stability and support provided by apparatus is invaluable for those lacking confidence and may even furnish the initial experience of what it is like to maintain inversion while moving onto, off or over the hands. On the apparatus the hands may move alternately, but not overtaking each other, as in swinging sideways along a bar, or one may pass the other as when the body travels in the forward and backward direction, Hanging, swinging and climbing are all activities which will answer this task.

Primary— Rope or other types of ladder, balance bars and climbing frames provide the children with opportunities for exploring the above ideas.

Middle and Secondary—Both boys and girls can experiment on bars at hanging height, travelling along and moving in all three directions, while some may also be able to travel up a rope or across a number of ropes taking weight on hands only. Boys, for physiological reasons, will probably be able to enjoy the challenge of swarming a rope or ladder using hands alone and will also produce a greater variety of methods of progressing along bars. This activity can occur on raised surfaces, parallel or inclined to the ground. The body can be pulled along the top or underneath with a number of bases being used.

Primary—Balance bars or planks inclined on to stools or raised between two stools, slippery topped tables or forms offer situations for pulling up, sliding along or down a variety of surfaces.

Middle and Secondary—This is not an activity that need to be pursued at any length but it can be dealt with adequately using inclined forms at a variety of heights and bars at hip level to give first years an experience of what is involved in the action.

Locomotion by rolling

If this action is to be attempted with confidence on apparatus, then it must be preceded by sufficient practice at floor level. The apparatus at first should be comparatively low, broad and stable and the individual can be expected to complete the roll on the apparatus provided, *i.e.* arrive on the apparatus, roll and then get off.

Primary—Table tops, wide planks, forms and stage blocks, are surfaces that can be used, provided they are not too high and are safe in all respects.

Middle and secondary— Children should be given the opportunity of experimenting with a variety of rolls on surfaces such as forms and box tops, and the majority should be able quite quickly to progress to some of the more difficult ways of rolling on apparatus, a point developed.

Locomotion by gripping and releasing alternately

This has already been mentioned with reference to travelling using hands only. In addition to this, however, children can be helped to explore other parts of the body capable of gripping, which can often be used in conjunction with hands to produce locomotion. These parts such as toes, instep, back of the knees and front of the hips cannot be included as weight bearing bases when travelling at floor level, but once on apparatus can, if necessary, support the whole weight of the body.

Primary—Any type of climbing frame, ropes or supported ladders and poles are suitable for children to experience the gripping action which is such a basic requirement for all work on apparatus.

Middle and secondary. Climbing frames, hinged wall bars, window ladders, bars, ropes, bar boxes and the horse pommels offer a variety of gripping situations.

In the early stages of planning apparatus for young children, the teacher's responsibility is to set the scene, providing an environment which will lead the children towards experiencing the greatest variety of activities possible. Provision should be made so that many of the above activities can be included, with each piece of apparatus dealing with a particular aspect of locomotion. Once the class begins to work on apparatus the teacher can help to widen the children's movement vocabulary by setting simple task that stimulate them to discover new ways of using the body when travelling. He must also ensure that each child is encouraged to work on several different pieces of apparatus and eventually tackles them all over a period of time. With older classes, apparatus can provide opportunities which include various methods of travelling, *e.g.* gripping and sliding, sliding and rolling, jumping over and rolling, while they can also be encouraged to travel over the apparatus using many pathways, travelling in a straight line, making a circular or zig-zag track.

Stillness

The body travelling and the body in stillness must both

be experienced if full awareness and skilful management are to be gained. Although in the early stages of mastering stillness It will suffice that movement is checked and body weight controlled, it should be realised that stillness does not merely mean "to stop moving". It implies that movement is held so that the muscular tension involved in arresting an action and maintaining a still position can be experienced. This should be considered as an active pause or a dynamic stillness rather than cessation of movement; a positive attitude should be adopted towards stillness in which appropriate tension is felt and used to maintain the position of the body.

Actions can be brought under control and stopped in several ways. If the body is kept compact and all angular parts contained within the curved shape, once the body is set in motion movement will be continuous until a time when the original momentum is lost. If, however, a flat part of the body is released, such as a forearm, and comes in contact with the floor, or the body itself is uncurled, movement will be interrupted. At that point, an abrupt stop can be achieved providing sufficient bodily tension can be produced to check the forward momentum at the moment when weight is;~ received on the flat part.

An abrupt stop is not always necessary, however, and stillness can be brought about by a gradual loss of momentum. When a landing from a jump which involves tilting or turning takes place, there may be a momentary loss of control and inability to halt the action unless the distribution of body weight is adjusted appropriately. One way of recovering equilibrium would be to continue to move, following the direction of body weight, and to round the body so that weight can quickly be transferred from feet to other parts. This may result in a rolling action where the speed can be controlled when the feet come into contact with the ground and grip the surface, or it may lead into a rocking motion where momentum can slowly decrease, resulting in eventual stillness.

Speed can be checked and a running action brought to a stop by ejecting the body into the air. In order to achieve the upward thrust at takeoff the forward lean of the body has to be altered. This opposing of the forward momentum by the vertical ejection is instrumental in initially checking the of the run. When considering the most effective way of stopping the action, it will be found that of the five basic jumps, the two to two is the most efficient. In a double take-off an initial interruption of speed occurs while one foot meets the other and the body is brought in to symmetry. On landing on two feet the body is more likely to be controlled and stable and an immediate stop can be effected in two ways. Firstly, movement can be checked through space when, on landing, the body flexes and regains the normal position w hile landing and recovery taking place on the same spot. Secondly, there can be a complete cessation of movement when a gripping action on arrival holds the landing position. The first method of stopping is the more usual and the resulting, resilience should be encouraged. The second is occasionally resorted to in some emergency landings, for example, where space is limited and also used in the more advanced aspects of flight into balance. In addition it is also a characteristic of landings from Olympic gymnastic vaults.

However, the more usual method of takeoff and landing is from one foot to two. In this instance the asymmetrical running action remains unaltered in the takeoff and it will not be until the feet come together in the air that symmetry is achieved, but ultimately this does take place and preparation can then be made for a two foot landing and, as previously stated, stillness may then result.

The stability and control achieved from a two foot landing obviously assists ultimate stillness. This may not be an immediate necessity and the performer may find it requires a, following jump or number of resilient jumps in order to control fully the momentum gathered in the preparation and the actual leap itself. In this case speed can be lost gradually, the height and tension involved in the bounces following the landing will decrease steadily until full control is experienced and a stop is made possible.

Movement can be performed with either free or bound flow. Free flow is apparent in movements which are difficult to stop at any given point, bound flow is evidenced when the control is such that actions can easily be checked. It will be recognised that in gymnastics free flow exists in certain ballistic situations but the attitide towards flow is mainly concerned with actions which are sufficiently controlled to allow for quick adjustment, adaptation or immediate stillness. In dealing with stillness it should be realised that the body control involved in achieving this is of great importance when considering safety in any movement situation.

Teaching

With young children, mastering stillness will be a

major step in managing body weight. They have little inclination to stop actions, being mainly concerned with travelling; in some instance: it is only due to the fact that they become exhausted that movement eventually ceases. In the early stages the teacher must be prepared to dictate the moment of stopping and yet not expect a common class response. Very few will be able to bring about anything but a gradual, cessation of movement. Another way of helping children to experience stopping is to set situations where a natural stop occurs, as in sliding, swivelling and spinning. This could be developed by helping them to contrast the feeling associated with the gradual petering out of movement in the actions, with a deliberate stopping of a slide or a spin ' an the resulting held position. The use of action phrases could prove effective at this stage, and words such as stop, check, balance, interrupt and arrive, contrasted with pause hover, rest, finish, decelerate, peter out and die away, used to produce variation, in the quality of *becoming* still. Later individuals can evolve their own phrases of movement and although this is a difficult stage, the teacher must be patient and persist, helping them to clarify the starting and final positions as well as paths followed and actions performed.

Once the initial stage of controlling the body has been mastered so that stillness results, children should be able to employ this ability in more difficult situations. They should become adept at avoiding obstacles and other children by stopping abruptly and be able to react to any situation requiring immediate stillness. It is at this stage that weight bearing on different parts may be introduced. If this is attempted before children have been given sufficient time to become accustomed to the tension which has to be produced before stillness is achieved, the result will be disappointing and little satisfaction will be experienced. Stillness here will involve a deliberate interruption the action and attention will be focused on the part or of the body bearing weight, rather than on the movements leading into and out of the arrival. There will be little or no feeling of the true balance or poise which will be developed when greater bodily skill has been mastered. The advanced technique involved in balance includes awareness of the manner in which the balance is achieved and lost..

The teacher of younger children is concerned more with action than stillness on apparatus, but the ability to stop or change direction to avoid others or obstacles is something that children must eventually learn to include in managing the body.

They can be helped to master the skill of checking movement by first experiencing the control required when changing direction. This can be accomplished with each child working individually on small apparatus.

Apparatus-individual mats.

Task.— Run and jump over the mat, turn and roil back.

Apparatus—a skipping rope on the floor.

Task.—Jump from side to side using feet only, at the end turn and come back using hands and feet to travel.

Apparatus—skittles and cane.

Task—Run and jump over the cane, turn and slide back underneath.

Inclined planks can also help children to control the impetus of movement, *e.g.* when travelling up a steeply inclined surface using feet only or hands and feet, the speed, naturally decelerates as the top is reached. As momentum' is lost the action becomes more easily controlled and a pause is quite simply effected. Similarly, when sliding down, a stop at the bottom is the usual result. Repetitive actions along forms, planks or benches can help the performer to appreciate phrasing and the child may, choose for himself how many times the action is to be repeated before stopping.

Older classes can be expected to perform slightly more difficult tasks such as showing moments of stillness during a sequence on apparatus or experimenting with the task of finding different ways of arriving and holding a position on a given piece of apparatus. Wall bars, climbing frame, ropes, bars, box and horse can be used in the latter case. Stillness should be seen as a contrast to locomotion and introduced in connection with travelling, but very soon the point at which the teacher can lead the class into weight, bearing will become apparent.

Weight bearing

Man's specialised way of using the body, that is, in the upright position, is not the main concern in gymnastics; the aim is to exploit the body to the full and to utilise it movement potential in a versatile manner. Weight bearing suggests that the weight of the body is above the supporting part; therefore on the floor weight bearing results in the body resting above a chosen base, although on apparatus, however, this is not necessarily the case. Locomotion and stillness are both related to this new idea because while travelling weight has to be controlled and held over the supporting part. Many parts of the body are capable of taking weight it will be discovered that some lend themselves more readily to producing a steady, stable base than others. The placement of these parts in relation to the floor and the rest of the body is also important. It appears natural in the early stages of weight bearing to use flat parts or parts that can be flattened such as shoulders, shins, hips, forearm and hands and to place these symmetrically.

As well as weight being equally distributed over two body parts which are the same, two or more different parts may be used which produce an equally steady base, *e.g.* a shin and hand, or a knee and two hands. The larger the base relative to the placement of the rest of the body, the steadier the position. It will be found when maintaining weight on two different parts that it is simpler to use right and left sides of the body. A progression will be to take weight on two different parts of the body using the same side, this requiring greater ability to control the body weight.

Later when greater skill has been acquired, the asymmetrical placing of parts can be exploited. Body weight can be held on a part of the trunk such as one hip or one shoulder, but a far more difficult challenge would be to produce an asymmetrical base using one or two limbs.

Rounded parts of the body can be used to support weight but when, for example, the head, knee or elbow forms part of the base other parts may be needed to stabilise the position. While maintaining weight on one or more parts, the rest of the body may remain still or may move. In a cartwheel, for example, the body weight is supported on the hands, while the *rest* of the body, extended, wheels over the support. While bearing weight on the shoulders the body may be still or moving over the base while another part is prepared to receive the weight.

Weight may be received and maintained on parts of the body for a brief period or can be held for a relatively longer time, while the freed parts of the body arc used, for example, readjusted to receive weight or to initiate the subsequent action. When taking weight either partially or wholly on the shoulders the legs may be symmetrical, reaching away from the ground, they may remain together or be far apart, one may bend and the other stretch, they may twist against the shoulders and circle, or one leg may reach out and the toe touch the floor whilst the other reaches up and away from the body.

Weight bearing must be considered in relation to body awareness: in the first instance the actual contact with he floor of different body parts heightens the kinesthetic sense; secondly, when weight is taken on parts not normally used, the rest of the body is placed in a completely new situation and learning to manage the body in this novel position presents a considerable physical challenge. When inverted, for example, reach and mobility alter and a complete re-orientation is necessary.

Finally, in the consideration of work on apparatus which requires negotiating different levels and using the body's full potential, awareness and ability to manage the body in any situation is seen to be invaluable.

Teaching

The child, having explored methods of travelling an mastered the skill involved in checking an action, can no' experiment with the idea that weight can be received on and supported by a number of different parts of the body. At first the teacher may need to help the class by suggesting that parts such as shoulders, hips and knees can bear the weight of the rest of the body. The children can then be encouraged to experiment for themselves, e.g. exploring the possibilities of weight bearing on all matching parts of the body, such as hands forearms, shins. These activities will be performed first in isolation but once the children have mastered a few possibilities, they can then be expected to attempt to link travelling and stopping with reference to weight bearing. At this point the teacher may have to refer back to the ways of travelling previously experienced, if, for example, the children limit themselves to using hands and feet only.

In order to extend the experience of bearing weight on two identical parts of the body it could be suggested that hands, for example, can be placed near together, farther apart side by side or one in front of the other.

A further progression might be to encourage the use of dissimilar parts of the body forming an asymmetrical base, and the class will probably produce many possibilities with this idea in mind.

Older children could be presented with the task of discovering isolated parts of the body on which weight can safely be taken, e.g. one hip, one shin or one shoulder, or experimenting with the possibility of producing uneven bases which not only requires a more skilful adjustment of the body over the base but also results in a more precarious position being experienced anticipating problems which be met later.

Movement habits are easily established at this Stage and it is here that the teacher can help children to experiment equally with right and left sides of the body so that weight received as often on one as on the other. Throughout this aspect of the work the teacher should emphasise that anticipation is needed so that parts which are to receive weight a' prepared in the previous movement. Most children natural prepare for action., this can be seen in the preparatory forward swing of the arms and backward movement of the top half of the body before attempting a handstand, and in the attitude adopted at the start of a race, or before measured jump.

Once children have become aware of the possibilities of weight bearing and have experienced a fair proportion, they can begin to give some attention to the ways in which the, rest of the body can be used while it is supported on any given base. Whilst weight is being borne on the hands, for example, the rest of the body can be elongated as in a hand-stand, it can be taken through a wide, stretched shape as in a cartwheel, it can be kept relatively compact as in a "Chinese" handstand, or crouch jump, or it can turn and twist in the air or move over the hands. These are only a few named skills and many others can be invented once the principle is grasped. It is of interest to note that the feet are high above the supporting hand whereas in all but two cases this is not so. During the exploratory stages of this idea, the child will, merely be resting on the weight bearing part. Later the teacher should make the point that the rest of the body produces the appropriate amount of tension, enabling the performer to feel that the body is held in position over point of contact with the floor. This is to ensure that the child maintains a liveliness within the body, alert to any action which might follow. Just as children's carriage is noted when in the normal positions of standing and sitting, so too, when weight is taken on other parts of the body, rather than allowing a collapse or slump, the teacher should encourage readiness, anticipation and a feeling of poise.

UP to this point the attention of the class will have been directed towards the part or parts of the body providing the base and the ability of the freed parts to be held or move in a variety of ways. When the child's attention becomes concerned with ways of arriving, as well as resulting action this leads naturally into consideration of methods of weight transference.

Apparatus

When apparatus is introduced not only has a variety surfaces and levels to be considered but also new parts of body can now take weight, different combinations of body parts can be used as supports and as previously noted body no longer needs to be above the supporting base.

Single apparatus

When providing apparatus situations for this theme it ii advisable to allow children time to work on single pieces of apparatus before confronting them with combinations. It is also helpful in the early stages to have the whole class using similar apparatus, e.g. everyone working on forms, or mats or a combination of bars and mats. Introducing this idea simply ensures that each child builds a considerable repertoire of ways of using single pieces of apparatus. This will be found of value later when groups are expected to work on a combination or circuit where forms, mats and bars', are used in conjunction with larger apparatus.

Apparatus—mats

Task 1.—Cross taking weight on the hands, return with weight on another part.

Task 2.—Approach with weight taken alternately on hands and feet, cross using parts of the trunk.

Apparatus—forms

Task1— Travel along the form with weight on hands, fee going from side to side.

Task2—Using one part of the body on the form another on the floor, travel from end to end.

Apparatus—bars

Task1—Experiment with ways of getting from one end the other using hands or feet or both.

Task 2.—Experiment with hanging positions where weight bearing parts are the highest.

Apparatus—window ladders.

Task1.—Travel up or across using hands and feet alter

Task 2.—Travel up or across using hands and a part of the body other than feet.

Apparatus—a low box.

Task1.— Move from one side to the other with one part only touching the apparatus, approach from any angle.

Task 2. Arrive on feet and get off with a part other than meeting the ground first.

Combinations of apparatus

The following are examples of combinations of apparatus which offer varying levels.

Apparatus—two ropes and a mattress.

*Task*1—Jump up onto one or both ropes; lower the feet gradually onto the floor. On contact with the floor transfer the weight on to other parts of the body such as knees, hips or shoulders.

Task 2— Preparation as in previous task but instead of lowering so that feet touch first, othér parts of the body make first contact with the floor.

Apparatus— bar (medium height), low box, mat.

Task.Hands must be used to lead the body from one piece of apparatus to the other, therefore they must be the first part of the body to contact each new piece of apparatus.

Apparatus—bar (hip height), saddle, bar box, mat.

Task.—A different part of the body must make first contact with each piece of apparatus.

Apparatus—ropes, low box, two mats.

Task.—Swing from one or two ropes and land on the box on different parts of the body. Hands must be the firs part to touch the mats.

Weight transference

In weight bearing the focus is directed towards the part or parts which are to receive weight and to the rest of the body while weight is being maintained on a specific part. In transference of weight the stress is on what happens between weight being removed from one part and arriving on another; in other words, how the body moves between two points of support. Whereas weight bearing is concerned with relative stillness, transference of weight involves locomotion. Although there is a correlation between transference of weight and locomotion, the emphasis in teaching is different, in locomotion it is on the travelling, getting from place to place, while in transference of weight it is on the transitional movement between two weight bearing positions.

Transference of weight may be brought about by any of four ways:

1. rocking and rolling,
2. sliding,
3. step-like actions,
4. flight

Rocking and rolling

This involves transference of weight on to adjacent body parts i,e. along the spine as in forward and backward rolls, across, the back as in sideways rolling, or on the front surface of the trunk. In some cases parts of the body which are not naturally adjacent can be made so. The feet can be brought near to the hips in a crouch position so that a movement where weight is transferred down the spine can be taken, without interruption, on to the heel and then the ball of the foot. The curved surface is thus maintained, allowing the rocking or rolling action already established to continue. Rocking differs slightly from rolling in that in rocking the weight is transferred on to adjacent parts and is brought back again along the same line of supports in reverse. In rolling the weight is transferred along the spine and then eventually taken on to another body part. Rocking leads very easily into rolling and vice versa.

Sliding

Sliding is another method whereby the body is transferred from one place to another while in constant contact with the supporting surface, but where it is not always true to say that weight has been transferred from one part to another. When children slide it is usually as a result of a run and dive, an in this instance the weight of the body is maintained on the same area, hips, side or front, while the body is carried along the ground. The initial impetus comes from the speed generated in the run and dive on to the floor and locomotion will continue until this energy is spent.

When the body is sliding on a comparatively large area other parts may be used to provide added propulsion but it is only incidental that they bear part of the weight of the body. In a sliding action on the hips the heels may be use intermittently to push and so maintain the original slide. While taking weight on the front surface of the body the hands, used alternately or together, can pull or push the body along the floor or apparatus and thereby assist the slide. Step-like transferences of weight resemble the process used in walking. In considering the walking action it can be seen that from standing on two feet, weight is shifted on to one whilst the other is lifted, prepared and placed in a new position. As weight is transferred on to the new support there is a moment when weight is equally distributed over the two feet, before being taken on to the foot last grounded and the process repeated, each foot overtaking the other in turn. Step-like transferences of weight can take place using a number of body parts, and in actions such as handstands and cartwheels this is the type of weight transference used, hands, and feet alternately acting as supports for the rest of the body.

Flight

Transference of weight by means of flight is usually made from feet to feet or feet to hands, but flight can be gained by using other parts of the body. In bouncing activities flight is achieved from, and weight received on to the same body part. Hands and feet can be used alternately with flight taking place between the push off from the feet and the landing on the hands or vice versa. This will be only momentary flight but the period in the air will be prolonged with the more skilful performer. Resilient landings, where the ability of the body to rebound is exploited, can be encouraged by bouncing and continuous leaping, while landing from a height and at speed may necessitate weight being transferred quickly on to another part. Use can be made here of the three other methods of weight transference.

Teaching

Although transference of weight is a fundamental gymnastic theme, it will depend upon the age and movement preference of the class where the teacher begins. With a class of beginners who are lively and energetic the starting point could be with flight and sliding, whereas when older children are being introduced to this type of work, the teacher would be well advised to begin with step-like transferences. Wherever the start is made, all four ways should be each following reasonably quickly upon the other.

Flight and Step-like actions involve the body in changing situations whereas once the body assumes the curled shape and begins rolling, no such changes occur until the action alters. The bodily situation remains comparatively unchanged in sliding also, once the action is begun. In teaching transference of weight, therefore, it is as well to cover two methods in one lesson if a balance of activity is to be achieved, e,g. rolling and step-like actions could be taken together or activities which include flight and sliding could be combined.

Rocking and rolling

Rocking on parts of the body suited to this activity is a good preparation for rolling as the appropriate surfaces will be discovered and the necessity for rounding these areas will be appreciated. When rocking on the back it can be pointed out that slight rocking can be produced when only a small area of the back is used, or a more vigorous action is possible if the weight is transferred along the length of the spine. If the feet are tucked in and made to produce a continuation of line with the back and hips, the rock can extend to the heel and ball of the foot and the movement can the continue in reverse. Children can experience rocking no only on to two feet placed side by side, but also on to two feet with one placed in front of the other. This the rocking action slightly and is useful gaining continuity of action in recovery. If, for example having completed a rocking action which is to be followed a cartwheel or a handstand, the feet are placed one of the other, this will lead the body more smoothly into these actions than if weight were to be equally distributed over the two.

One activity which children might practise is rocking forwards and backwards on the back, gradually gaining momentum and including the feet in the action. When sufficient energy and speed have been gathered, the forward momentum can be directed either into a handstand or crouch jump or can be used to eject the body into the air. Having introduced the possibility that weight can be transferred on to feet at the completion of a rocking action, the child can now experiment with the idea that as the feet or the shoulders receive weight, the rest of the body is free to be redirected by a slight twist of the top or lower half against the fixed part.

Children should experience both curving and arching the spine and having discovered the possibilities of rocking on,: the back, the front surface of the body should be used. Some will find rocking along the front of the body, transferring the weight from the chest to the hips, quite difficult as this requires considerable strength and mobility. Once they have felt the two extremes of curling and arching the spine, some children will find this useful on apparatus, The active use of the upper and lower half of the body in, this method of rocking should be encouraged and ways leading into and twisting out of this action can be discovered.

A rocking action can also be effected by using the back from right to left of the spine, resulting in a side to side movement. The body, in this case, can be elongated or curled. The arms should be tucked in and the front of the body contracted so that the shoulders and back are rounded as much as possible, allowing maximum rocking to take place across the whole area. Once this has been mastered, ways of getting into and out of this position by transferring weight on to parts such as knees, forearms and hands can be explored

Within rocking, the speed changes and the pauses which occur before a change of direction give the child valuable experience in that he can learn to increase and decrease momentum and discover the resulting rhythms, whilst the hesitation felt as the rocking action reaches the end of its path is perhaps a new experience for most. It is when performing, such actions that children begin to appreciate inherent time stresses. It can also provide them with background knowledge which can be used to advantage at a later stage changes of speed within actions are considered. With younger classes and to some extent with older children, this not be so—it may not involve them in a conscious awareness—but if the teacher understands and gives the children bodily experience, this is sufficient until such time as they become capable of coping conceptually.

Although in pre-school play most children will probably have experienced rolling, they will not necessarily have explored all the possibilities. As a safety precaution the teacher needs to stress that in rolling the body as a whole must also curled, presenting a rounded surface to the floor. It should also be pointed out that all angular parts must be brought within the compact, curved shape of the body.

The head is an extension of the spine and as such must be included as part of the curve made by the rest of the body. Making this point to children attempting a forward roll will help most of them to achieve the skill smoothly and safely. Often when rolling children drop on to the back, which has been flattened as a result of the head instead of the shoulders first taking the weight. This can usually be overcome if the teacher leads the children to experience curving the spine and tucking the head while remaining in a crouch position on the feet. If, from this position, the hips are lifted and the feet Push slightly, the head looking into the space between the legs, a roll will result. Others may find a roll over one shoulder easier and this can be achieved if, for example, fro a position on all fours, the left hand is released and, with the head following, leads the body through the space made by, the remaining hand and the knees. As the left shoulder, comes level with the right knee, a state of unbalance occurs,' and if weight is then taken on to this shoulder, an asymmetrical roll follows.

Some children will prefer rolling backwards over a shoulder, for once the hips are lifted off the ground and one or both knees directed over one shoulder, the weight is such that the rest of the body easily follows and a roll is achieved. For those who do not feel sufficiently confident to attempt any of these ways, rolling with the body either in a ball shape or elongated, will be their first experience of continuous movement using this method of weight transference.

Another method of helping children to roll is to suggest they use the experience previously gained in rocking. Rocking on the back, for example, can lead quite easily, for some, into either a forward or backward roll, where the body shape remains constant. For those who quickly master rolling itself, combining rocking and rolling and exploring all the possibilities of rocking into and out of a roll provides a different challenge.

If the teacher suggests that rolling can be performed in a number of different ways and allows the class complete freedom to practise rolls already mastered, or to discover new ways of rolling, each child is able to attempt the way or ways he finds easiest. It is then left to the teacher, knowing all the possibilities and ways of achieving them, to lead the class or individuals gradually towards an appreciation of what is involved in rolling. Young children gain satisfaction from repetitive action and during the exploratory period it could be suggested that consecutive rolls are attempted. Man enjoy this activity, discovering that the rolls can take place within a limited area, i.e. a backward roll followed by forward roll, or that travelling occurs when rolls are performed consecutively.

The more able the performer the greater the variety he should achieve, but each child, whatever stage he has reached should be encouraged to perform asymmetrical rolls using right and left sides equally. Although most individuals have a preference for one side or the other, the ability to roll over either shoulder is of value later, particularly when performing a series of actions on apparatus or when working with a partner. If sufficient mats are available when children begin work on rocking and rolling these should be used in the early stages, but as the action itself becomes more efficient and the children more confident, the necessity for mats diminishes and the tendency to limit the performer avoided. Care is always needed whenever children roll without mats and these should always be provided when using apparatus.

When children have become reasonably proficient their skill level can be raised by introducing a variety of specific tasks such as those which follow.

Task 1.—Lie face downward and, with the body elongated, slide into a forward roll.

Task 2.—Lie on the back with legs together and stretched; maintaining this elongated position of the legs through-out, lift the legs and direct them backward towards the floor immediately behind the head; once contact is made resolve the roll by a sliding action which culminates in the body coming to rest face downward.

Task 3–Explore the possible combinations of tucking, elongating, stretching, twisting and arching, for example

—begin with legs astride, roll either forward or backward ending with the body tucked, or

— begin facing one direction; roll and prior to completing the roll effect a change of direction using a twist and perhaps arriving on a shin with the free leg extended.

Task 4.—Roll into and out of a handstand or headstand.

Task 5.—Rock on the front surface of the trunk into a one shoulder balance and roll out along or across the back.

Task 6.—Roll backward onto one shoulder and rock out along the front surface of the trunk.

Sliding

Although sliding is an activity which most children will have encountered it will usually have been associated with inclined surfaces. It can, however, be experienced on the floor provided that it is clean and splinter free. This is an important point whenever children are working but ever more so when the action involves friction.

The class should first experiment with actions which naturally terminate in sliding, e.g. when starting from, position on the floor with weight on hips, a vigorous pushing action of the feet against the floor will set the slide in motion. A more effective push, resulting in a longer sliding action, becomes possible if the weight is taken on the feet body curled, and only when the legs become extended is weight transferred to the hips. Junior children are remarkably skilful at launching themselves on to the floor and into a slide. This can be experienced from a standing position or, as happens more naturally, from a run.

While experimenting with actions which result in sliding, children incidentally discover that many areas of the trunk can be used. They can begin to combine the pulling and pushing action of the limbs with taking weight on different parts of the trunk, e.g. the weight can be taken on the front surface of the trunk and the hands used to pull and then push the body into a slide or, with weight on the hips, the hands and feet can push the body into action. The more proficient children are, the greater the variety achieved. Most boys become expert at launching themselves on to the hips, front, side and thighs.

Some children naturally appreciate that the body travels better if it is streamlined and weight is taken on a comparatively small area. The teacher can help others to discover this by suggesting that they slide with whole surfaces of the body contacting the floor and then only part of this surface maintaining the body weight. In the latter instance the appropriate degree of bodily tension must be produced to hold the non-sliding parts off the ground.

Step-like actions

In step-like transferences many non-adjacent parts of the body can receive weight in turn. In rocking and rolling the child is concerned with large areas of the trunk along or across which weight is continually being transferred; now his attention is drawn to isolated parts of the whole body, and the combinations possible when using them in succession to produce locomotion.

It should be appreciated that in rocking and rolling movement will be continuous throughout the action. Step-like transferences may involve an interruption in the continuity of the action when weight is transferred on to flat or flattened parts of the body and maintained over that part for a brief period. This does not occur when the performer becomes more competent and able to repeat actions with and fluency. The teacher should also realise that by the very nature of rocking and rolling activities, since adjacent parts are used in immediate succession, no variety of weight bearing parts is possible within one action. Step-like transferences, however, involve choice and therefore selection is necessary. It should be pointed out to the class that parts can be placed close to each other, as when transferring weight from feet to hands in hand balance, or comparatively far away, as in a cartwheel. When the part which is being prepared to receive weight is to be placed to the side or a long way away from supporting part, a considerable amount of bodily adjustment is involved, and great control is required before these skills are performed with any degree of fluency.

In some actions weight is taken from one part, received on another and placed back again on to the original part, as in handstands and cartwheels. Other actions can be accomplished which involve a constant change of parts transferences using hands and feet many variations are possible when combining the four limbs. The children should be allowed time to experiment, e.g. with transferring weight from two feet to two hands, two feet to one hand or from two hands to one foot. It is when dealing with step-like transferences of weight that the teacher should ensure that weight is taken frequently on the hands and in many differing situations. At an early stage children should be helped and encouraged to become increasingly confident in the inverted position. Tasks such as the following are challenges which will eventually lead most children towards becoming both competent and confident on the hands in inverted positions.

Task 1.—Take weight on to hands and make the legs land in a new place. Land one foot after the other or two feet together.

Task 2.—Take weight on the hands and get one foot high into the air.

Task 3.—Take weight on the hands and make one foot pass the other in the air.

Task 4.—Take weight on the hands and make the feet meet at some point in the air.

This method of transferring weight requires a studied, deliberate action on the part of the performer, and means that the child must think in advance of the action he is performing.

Flight

Jumping is an activity which the majority of children will have experienced previously as a means of travelling, but when flight is being introduced as one of the ways of transferring weight some of the considerations which are involved in flight must be dealt with.

With young juniors it is sufficient that they play with the various ways already used earlier, such as hopping, skipping, bounding and leaping. Later the teacher can make the class aware that the feet can be used singly or together in both takeoff and landing; that feet can catch each other up as in a single takeoff with two feet landing, or that feet can pass as in leaping from one foot to the other. Together with bouncing along on two feet or one foot these activities will involve them, incidentally, in the five basic jumps. At this stage it is the going away from and meeting the floor again that is emphasised, not being in the air.

The next stage will be to introduce the idea that individual parts of the limbs can be stressed after take-off, e.g. knees can be accentuated when the legs become freed, one or both this can be done be tucked up towards the chest and this can be done together or one after the other; feet can be lifted high into the air in front of the body one after the other, kicked into the space behind, or brought to the side. It will be appreciated that although this task will result in a variety of body shapes being assumed in the air, shape itself has not been stressed. At this stage it is incidental and the attention of the class is directed towards awareness and use of different body parts.

In the early stages of flight the accent should be on resiliency, as children are, on the whole, naturally more concerned with producing a succession of actions such as skipping or hopping. They enjoy experimenting with parts of the body other than feet on which they can bounce, and are prepared to choose activities involving shins, hips and shoulders. Bouncing, combining body parts such as hand and feet, can also be explored by some.

Within the jumping action the body spends such a comparatively short time in the air that the landing often occurs before any specific preparation or conscious effort can be made. In the transference of weight on to hands and feet, as in repetitive crouch jumps, the feet, which are usually both the ejectors and receivers of weight, are allowed more time in the air to prepare for the landing; consequently attention can be paid to meeting the floor. This "slow motion" effect of landing, for some, will be the experience they will find most valuable when considering the landing action. Weight should be received on to two feet or the feet used one after the other on landing, assuring equal efficiency in both methods of landing. As children become more proficient in flight and able to combine a variety of ways of transferring weight, e.g. run, jump, land and roll, they can be expected to produce appropriate ways of landing.

It is in the first two years with juniors or the first year in the Secondary school that children should become thoroughly familiar with and skilful in ways of using the feet in takeoff and landing. They should also have been given guidance in efficient ways of landing so that they feel confident in jumping from a variety of heights. Although the principles of landing are common to all, the teacher should be particularly aware of children who, through habit, lack of control or fear, land awkwardly. These individuals are always liable to have accidents, particularly as the flight becomes varied. Some children land with the feet wide apart, which could lead to damage to the knee. Others land with one or both feet slightly inturned, making ankle and knee liable to injury. A few children tend to assist landing on the feet with one or both hands, probably a continuation of young children's liking for landing on all fours. This could be dangerous, particularly when the weight is not directly over the feet and the hands are placed in front or behind in a misguided attempt to counteract the natural momentum an direction of the falling body. It is very difficult to break such habit actions so the teacher must deal with them promptly, before they become well established. These children need individual help and constant reminding of what they must do to correct such faults whenever landings occur in a lesson.

It is only by steering the children progressively through these early stages that the confidence required for the more advanced work will be gained and a real enjoyment of flight becomes possible.

Although the teacher will guide his class through all the methods of transferring weight, only in the very early stages will these actions be performed in isolation. As soon as he feels the class capable of managing the body safely using one method two ways of transferring weight at least should be combined. If, as previously suggested, rocking and rolling, flight and sliding are introduced simultaneously, then choosing other appropriate ways is a natural progression.

With more experienced children the teacher should aim to foster the ability to build sequences, selected from the variety discovered, and to perform any combination of actions fluently.

Apparatus

Work on apparatus challenges the children to perform types of action experienced on the floor at a variety of levels and on different surfaces, and to choose the appropriate method of transference of weight, so that movement over the apparatus becomes a logical and efficient way of travelling.

With juniors just beginning this work, each method of weight transference should be explored separately. Apparatus should be provided where sliding, for example, is the activity which is emphasised, and although in order to slide down they must first climb up, sliding is the main action with which the teacher helps them to experiment. Climbing apparatus such as rope ladders, scrambling nets or wallbars allows the group to explore step-like transferences of weight. Although the hands and feet are naturally used when Climbing, the class should be encouraged to try gripping with other parts. Juniors will provide a great variety of answers to the problem of showing flight either on or off or over apparatus. The teacher should help by ensuring that the apparatus is not too high at first. Where this is impossible, an inclined approach could be provided. He can suggest various ways of approach and encourage the group to use a number of different body parts to bear weight while fulfilling the task.

The following tasks on apparatus could be given to a class who have just begun this work and need to experiment with each of the methods of transferring weight.

Apparatus—low table, or box top or form.

Task.—Find different ways to get on and off or over.

Apparatus—two inclined forms on stools, with a linking bar. '*Task.* Experiment with different ways of sliding up and down the inclined forms and along the bar either on top or underneath.

Apparatus—climbing frame.

Task.—Climb up, travel along and climb down, showing weight bearing on at least three different body parts.

Apparatus-steps or stage blocks.

Task— Jump on and off or over.

Apparatus—mats.

Task—Free practice in rolling, showing variety.

Apparatus—a series of canes supported on skittles.

Task— Alternately jump over and slide or roll únder.

When considering apparatus for actions involving the transference of weight, the teacher should bear in mind that the four methods of weight transference can seldom be considered in absolute isolation. The following headings therefore consider two of the more usual combinations. The linking of like actions as in rocking and rolling should be taught first, as the transition is comparatively simple. Later, other combinations which include joining unlike, actions, involving change of level for example, as in flight and rolling, can be attempted.

Rocking and rolling

These two actions can be performed over a low bar, on forms or low box top. It may be found that to cover the bar with a mat will provide a more comfortable surface on which to rock. The children can find ways of rolling along a form, forwards and backwards. They can experiment, using feet on the, floor astride the form while the trunk rolls along the form, and complete the whole action with the body at the same level. The possibilities and advantages of rocking into rolling can also be explored. This activity will involve the performer in skilfully balancing and controlling the body on the"~ narrow surface provided by the form.

Apparatus—low box top, mats.

Task 1.—Get on to the box, roll along the top and jump off. Cross the mat using a different type of roll.

*Task*2.—Get on to the box, roll along and off, and roll again on the mat.

Task 3.—Go straight from the floor into a roll on the box, rock off into a roll.

In the first task the roll will be completed on the same level, whereas in the second and third either the take-off or the completion will be on a different level from the roll itself.

Step-like actions and flight

Getting on to apparatus at first usually involves step-like in order to gain height so that flight may follow.

Using fixed wall bars, window ladders and double bars or any kind of climbing apparatus, the tasks could be to climb up and jump down, or climb up, get through and jump down, The transferences here include negotiating comparatively small, vertical gaps. The children could also be expected to cover narrow, horizontal gaps where the level remains the same, e.g. two forms or two low box tops.

Apparatus such as the horse, box, buck or bar box can be used to get on using step-like transferences and get off by means of flight.

Flight and rolling

Rolling will have been practised at many of the earlier stages and can now be linked with landing from a jump. This necessitates an ability to move fluently from high to low level and involves a quick adjustment of body weight. It is, however, an essential skill and the class should be encouraged to explore with apparatus at a low height:

1. landing and rolling in the same direction as the body weight this can be experienced jumping forwards, backwards, sideways and with the body turning;
2. landing and rocking,
3. landing, controlling the body weight and redirecting the body into a roll.

The first two methods are the more usual and children should learn to feel where the body weight is on landing and act accordingly. Occasionally it is impossible to follow the natural direction, because of obstacles in the pathway of the mover, and the performer may be forced to resort to the third method.

It will be obvious from the above examples that many other natural combinations of transferring weight can be used, such as sliding into rolling, and step-like transferences into sliding. Eventually the class should be able to combine three or even all methods when using apparatus, if this has been arranged thoughtfully and with the theme in mind. The following examples could be used with children who have already been introduced to this movement idea and have experimented as suggested above.

Apparatus—an inclined form to a hinged side wall and a mat.

Task.—Starting point A: a sliding action up the form; get through, along and jump down, roll over the mat. Starting point B: roll over the mat, climb up, travel along, get through and slide down.

Apparatus-bar box, two forms, two mats.

Task.—A, B and C show possible starting points. Take any starting point and using at least three pieces of apparatus show three different methods ·of transferring weight.

Apparatus—horse and two mats

Task.—A, B and C are possible starting points. Approach from any angle, arrive on different body parts and get off using step-like actions; roll over mats.

Apparatus—a form inclined to a wall bar, two mats.

Task.—Use the apparatus and include at least three ways of, transferring weight.

Apparatus—a high bar and mats.

Task.—Starting point A. Travel along the bar, using step-like and sliding actions, up flight to get off and a roll on the mat.

Apparatus—box, medium height

Task.—Approach from any angle using a step-like transference to get on, and flight to get off.

Apparatus—low box and mattress.

Task. —Run, jump on to and off or over the box, land roll.

Apparatus—horse, box and two mats.

Task.— Include three ways of transferring weight within a sequence, using all the apparatus.

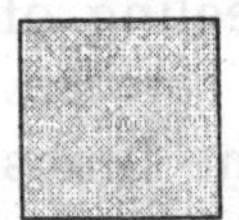

INTERMEDIATE BODY MANAGEMENT

In intermediate body management, however, the attention shifts to considerations of stretching and curling, twisting and turning and symmetry and asymmetry where the concern is with the body as a whole and locomotion and stillness become incidental. When children are aware of the variety of travelling possibilities and have become familiar with ways of taking weight and transferring weight, the changing shape of the body whilst it is moving can be explored. The comparatively simple actions of curling and stretching will have been performed already many times, but the attention may well have been directed towards other problems.

Flexion and extension are integral parts of any action and common to all movement. Curling and stretching are movements which are possible because of the flexible structure of the spine and both are related to a centre, which in whole body movement would be the centre of the body. Stress differs, however, in that in curling it is to close around this area whilst in stretching the main aim is to reach out and away from it. In some instances, however, the pull away will be related to the base in addition to a centre as such. The stretching of the body when lying or standing in an elongated position will be equally stressed in both the upper and lower halves, away from the central region, whereas the stretch experienced in a handstand will be felt as a pushing away from hands or base, although the feeling of reaching away from the centre should remain. Stretching can also be experienced with the limbs spread, emphasising breadth, as in a cartwheel.

Hyperextension of the spine results in the body arching, and this can produce backward or lateral movements with one half of the body stretching while the other naturally compensates by contracting. In backward arching the front surface is extended while the back contracts, whereas when the sideways arch is achieved, it is one side of the body which stretched while the other becomes compressed.

Teaching

In all the previous ways of moving the body will have alternated between these two actions. Reference will have been made many times to both curling and stretching when roking and rolling, while stretching will probably have been enouraged when dealing with certain aspects of flight. For a brief period it may be found valuable for children to experience the two extremes possible within this movement, in positions of stillness. Having to concentrate on rounding and elongating the spine and feeling its resulting effect on the whole body is useful as these two activities are obviously initiated in the trunk and awareness of this area is often neglected. Children should be guided towards feeling the positions of curled and stretched and also the process of *'becoming* curled and stretched, appreciating the difference between "I am *stretched*" and "I am *stretching*".

If stretched and curled positions are achieved as the natural conclusion of stretching or curling actions, they can be of value in experiencing the ultimate. If children are merely expected to produce isolated stretched or curled positions the results will be relatively useless. It is the interplay and compensatory reactions of the body moving into and between curled and stretched positions that should be experienced. Static positions unrelated to each other are of little value, but the feeling of stretching and the differing sensation experienced in curling, and moving from one to the other, are the important factors to be considered. Some of the justifiable criticisms levelled against the results of lessons with this theme as their focus might well be avoided if teachers were to recognise the full implications of the previous sentence.

It should be realised at this juncture that in the action of stretching the body can be elongated, stressing the upper and lower halves reaching in opposite directions, or it can be wide, accentuating the right and left sides pulling away from the central line, the spine. In the very early stages of stretching or curling the trunk should be made the most important part of the body, as children readily achieve, extension and flexion in the limbs but find mobility of the trunk a much more difficult task. The head, too, should be included in both these actions whether it is regarded as part, of the trunk and an extension of the spine, or looked upon as another limb.

When children are being led through these first experiences it is probably better for the teacher to suggest parts of the body which might take weight. It should be realised that only in positions of lying, standing on either toes or hands, and in the air, can a complete stretch be made, while curled positions can occur on feet, shins, either side and any part of the back. The whole class could quite quickly explore most of these possibilities, the majority being capable of experiencing all.

Having felt the extremes of curling and stretching with the body supported on bases selected by the teacher, the children can now experiment with other bases, symmetrical i and asymmetrical, over which the rest of the body can: extend or curl. It will be found that only an incomplete stretch is possible once the weight is taken on the shoulders or certain other parts of the body. Even so, when these bases are used the teacher should stress that the part capable of stretching should do so to the full. Similarly, in curling it will be discovered that on certain bases one part of necessity will need to be extended, although the majority of body parts will be able to curl over this base.

The ability of the spine to curve and arch backward,forwards and laterally must be exploited if true versatility and mobility are to be achieved. Often curling results only in forward and backward rolling actions, whereas if children are encouraged to experiment with the idea that the spine is capable of arching backwards and sideways, not only will a greater variety of ideas result but also a more skilful response will be demanded.

Most of this work will have been achieved statically and soon travelling should be stressed, as this necessitates weight being taken on various body parts, which will help the performer to experience leading into, moving through and resolving actions where the body is stretched or curled. The relation and interdependence of the two actions will also need to be understood: that in order to extend, a preparatory flexion is required, and that the natural reaction after a complete stretch is for the body to recover by contracting.

Travelling will probably include flight and it is here that the teacher should realise the difficulties involved in curling when airborne. It is much simpler to stretch in the air as, after take-off and in preparation for landing, the legs are already extended, while in an upward thrust the upper half of 'body is automatically affected in the attempt to overcome gravity. Thus the reaction of the body would seem to tend towards extension in the air and all the ways of stretching should be explored first before experimenting with curling the body in flight. Most children will find this difficult to achieve, as it involves a complete action taking place after take-off and before meeting the floor, and a deterioration in landing might result. It may be that the teacher will prefer to postpone this stage and deal with it later in advanced flight.

Apparatus

In the planning of apparatus for this theme the normal ways of using the body should be considered, i.e. flexion usually both precedes and follows extension, the actions of curling and stretching thus alternating. It would be pointless to expect children to travel over several pieces of apparatus Maintaining either a curled or stretched position, but the teacher should guide them to explore the many possibilities of stretching and curling according to the situations presented. It will soon be realised that in an action where the body is first curled and then extended, parts of the body may be stretched while others remain tucked. For example, one part may be gripping the apparatus while the freed part reaches out to receive weight, as when swinging on a rope where the arms are flexed and the legs prep to land, or when climbing a rope where the upper and low limbs work alternately gripping, reaching, pulling and pushing.

Young children can work with raised canes individual mats and skipping ropes on the floor or large mats, before introducing work on larger apparatus.

Apparatus—two individual mats

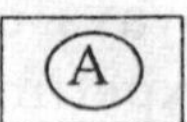

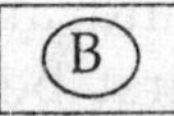

Task—Cross A keeping the body curled, cross B stretching. Find your own way of joining the two movements.

Apparatus—two individual mats and two skipping ropes.

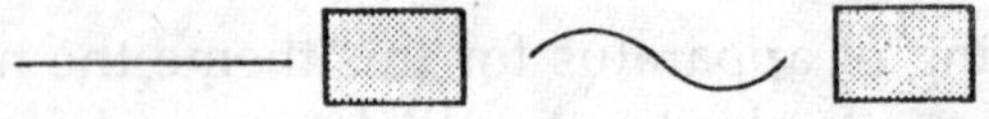

*Task.*Travel across the mats keeping the body curled, travel over the ropes going from side to side with weight on hands and the rest of the body alternately stretching and curling.

Apparatus—raised canes and hoops.

Task.—Travel in, out and over, stretching and curling

Forms and mats can be used with either beginners or m experienced classes.

Apparatus—a form used broadways.

Task.—Travel across the form keeping the body tucked an return showing a stretch or arch.

Appratus—a form used lengthways and a mat.

Task—Travel along the form alternately stretching and curling. Jump off the end and roll over the mat.

Apparatus—a bar at hanging height.

Task— Travel along either stretching or alternately stretching and curling

Apparatus—a low bar.

Task— Travel along jumping over and returning by rolling over or under.

Apparatus—ropes.

Task—1—Travel up.

Task2—Using one or two ropes explore the possibilities of changing shape whilst the ropes are still or moving.

Apparatus—climbing frame, window ladders or double bars.

Task—Travel up and down, over or across with the body alternately stretching and curling.

Apparatus—box top or two layers of the box and mats.

Task— Arrive on using hands and feet; get off with hands touching the mat first.

Apparatus—horse and mats, starting points A and B.

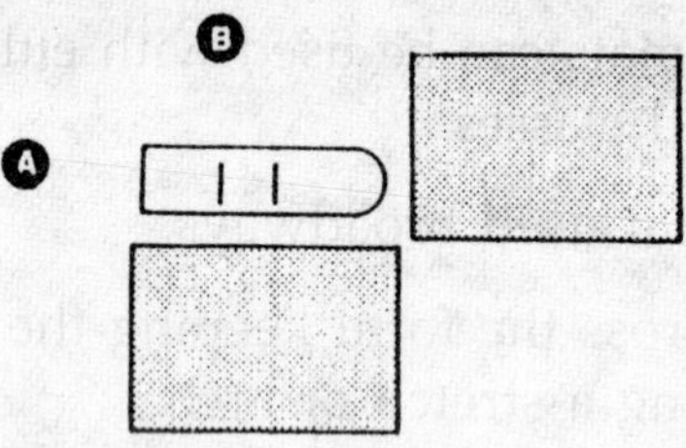

Task.—Arrive on and get off by taking weight on hands arid achieving a stretch to land. Roll over either of the mats.

When children have had sufficient time to experiment single pieces of apparatus, they can be presented with a in complicated arrangement where they explore curling stretching possibilities before selecting a series of actions be the basis of a sequence.

Apparatus—two forms, a buck and two mats,

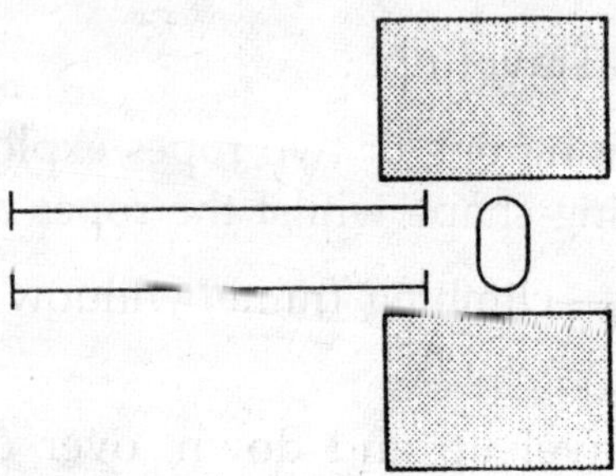

Apparatus—one form, two ropes and a box.

Apparatus—two bars, two inclined forms on the lower bar, two saddles and two mats.

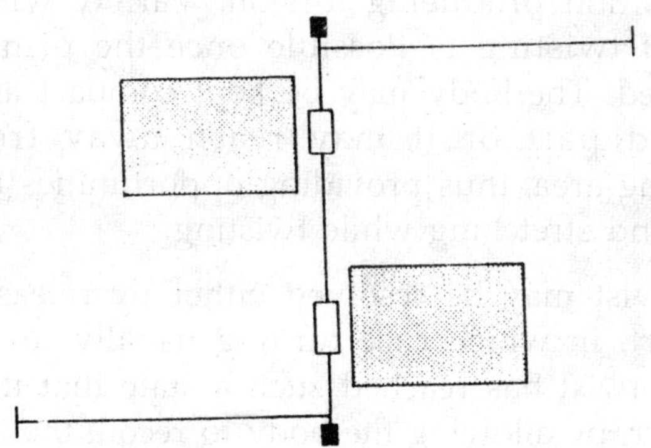

Apparatus—inclined form to a bar box, a horse with one pommel two mats.

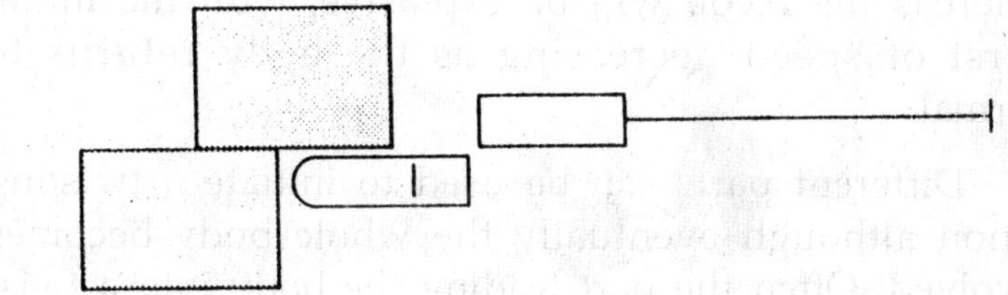

Twisting and turning

Two further actions of which the body is capable are those of twisting and turning. Twisting is made possible because of the jointed nature of the body and if increased mobility is to be achieved then the variety of additional gymnastic actions which result from work on this theme needs to be thoroughly explored and the principles understood.

Twisting occurs when one body part is stabilised and the rest of the body screwed so that different surfaces face different fronts, i.e. parts of the body act in opposition producing torsion. Variety within the action of twisting is Possible once the principle is established. The body may be kept compact and near the fixed part or it may reach away from the supporting area, thus providing opportunities for both curling and stretching while twisting.

A twist may be resolved either by releasing the fixed part, in which case turning usually results, or, once the twist has reached such a state that it can go no further, by allowing the body to recoil, the inherent speed changes involved in twisting becoming apparent. It will be found that movements leading into twisting are usually performed comparatively slowly, decreasing as the ultimate twisted state is reached, whereas the recoil will be explosive, with the initial burst of speed decreasing as the body returns to normal.

Different parts can be used to initiate a twisting action although eventually the whole body becomes involved. Often the part leading the body into a twist is the part that eventually takes and maintains weight. An effective way preparing for a twisting action is to screw the body in the opposite direction first, when the release of tension result in added impetus to the main action.

Turning concerns the body as a whole rotating at right angles about one of three possible axes the up-down vertical axis, and the two horizontal axes—the side to side a the forward—backward. Actions resulting from the body revolving around the vertical axis are those such as rolling with the body maintaining an elongated position, spinning on the hips, turning jumps, or making quarter or half turns fro a balance on hands. Forward and backward rolls arc' examples of the body rotating round the side to side axis, while moving through an inverted balance into an arch is an instance where the revolution is only half completed. A cartwheel will be recognised as an action where the rotation of the body is around the forward backward axis. Angular flight, that is flight involving rotation, can be achieved not only in turning jumps about the vertical axis, rotation can occur around all three axes and result, for example, in aerial somersaults or can involve rotation about two axes when twists are incorporated.

Pivoting swivelling and spinning are actions which involve turning and can be seen as similar in some respects to sliding. Pivoting suggests that impetus is recharged intermittently by a further action of a body part other than that taking the main weight. Swivelling or spinning occur when the initial action, only is used to maintain the motion, which will eventually lose momentum and come to an end. The speed of the body can be varied to some extent in all these actions by the shape it assumes while rotating—a compact body will revolve at greater speed than when the body is spread. The surface areas used in pivoting, swivelling and spinning can be the same as in sliding. The flow of the movement in all sliding actions, whether on the spot or travelling, may be less bound than in many other gymnastic activities and provide moments when comparative free flow can be experienced and enjoyed.

Whereas turning is concerned with the body as a whole, twisting involves awareness of parts within the whole acting against each other. The fact that the body moves as a unit in turning permits simultaneous action only, whereas in twisting body parts are used successively, joints coming into action one after the other.

Unless use is made of twisting and turning actions the performer is limited to movement in the forward backward and up-down directions. Twisting in isolation can result in static contorted positions being achieved with no further aim in view, but if the ability of the body to twist is exploited gymnastically then the action becomes purposeful.

In curling, stretching, twisting and turning the body is used to the fullest extent and if versatility is to be fostered all must be explored in depth. The ability to move fluently and with awareness, using these four actions appropriately both on the floor and on apparatus, is not easy to achieve, but when developed provides the performer with a very much wider range of activity.

Teaching

As with curling and stretching, if the teacher directs

the initial experiences he can ensure that each child understands some of the fundamental principles involved within the action. There is little point in twisting into a position only to resolve it along the same pathway, and teachers should ensure from the outset that a twist is used functionally in so far as it can be used, for example, to:

change direction,

transfer weight, or

gain initial impetus for a turning action.

The following tasks place children in situations where the body twist is resolved with the focus on transference of weight..

Task 1.—Start in a crouch position with weight on the feet, which are kept fixed. Use the hands to walk~ round the base until a position is reached where they can go no farther. Take weight on to the hands, release the feet and ground them again in a different place.

Task 2.—Begin with weight on the shoulders with the legs extended symmetrically above the base. Draw both knees down over either the right or left shoulder and transfer weight, ending in a kneeling position.

Task 3.—Take up a kneeling position and place one hand on the floor. Allow the other hand to lead the body into the space between the fixed hand and the knees. Transfer weight on to one shoulder and either roll or maintain the weight over this base.

The class could now be given the task of discovering new ways of transferring weight from feet to hands and, by twisting bringing the feet down in a different place. Here each child will solve the task in his own way and results may from asymmetrical crouch jumps to variations of hand-stands and cartwheels with twists. Using their previous experience of rocking, some could now experiment with ways of twisting out of front rocking, where it will be discovered that if a quick twist is used either at the beginning or end of the action, weight can be transferred on to the back. The twist will occur when the weight is on the upper half of the body and the lower half is free to twist against it or vice versa.

Twisting can be combined with curling or stretching, when the body screws downwards towards the supporting base or the part which is eventually to take weight reaches away from the support.

In turning the possibilities are varied but actions such as rolling will have already been experienced. This leaves only 'wheeling, spinning and aerial rotation as new activities to be explored. The former is limited to actions where weight is borne alternately on the hands and feet with the body wheeling over successive supports and children should be given a brief experience of this way of turning. The resulting actions will develop, for some, into cartwheeling, for others, into unnamed wheeling skills. Spinning, swivelling and pivoting on different parts of the body can be explored, with the children being encouraged to use twisting as a preparation for these activities. Angular flight about the horizontal axis and flight involving both twisting and turning may be achieved only by the more able performers who attend the school gymnastic club or classes organised by other bodies. Nevertheless those who are capable of producing, for example, aerial somersaults, cartwheels or walkovers should be encouraged to practise and perfect these skills and include them, when appropriate, in sequential work. Twisting and turning are easily linked as one often either precedes or results from the other. The opportunity to explore all the possibilities offered by both in gymnastics results eventually in the body being used in a skilful and versatile way.

Apparatus

Children need to be reasonably competent before this theme is introduced since the changes of orientation which have to be accommodated while the body twists and turns on apparatus should not be underestimated.

Apparatus—mats and forms.

Task 1—Grip the form and by releasing the lower limbs bring about a twist and a change of direction; on landing fix the feet and allow the upper half to initiate the twist, and take the body weight. Repeat this travelling along the form.

Task 2.—Experiment with fixing other body parts on the apparatus and bring about twisting.

The teacher can, if necessary, suggest parts of the body to fix and encourage the use of the different levels provide by the form and the floor.

Apparatus—junior frames, wallbars both hinged and fixed window ladders and single and double bars.

Task1—Experiment with fixing parts of the body by means of gripping, e.g. parts of the foot, the back of the knee, the front of the hips, and waist.

Task 2.—Travel up and down, along or across with a repetitive twisting action.

Task 3.—Experiment with a variety of ways of rolling around the bars; include rotation around the three axes.

Apparatus—ropes.

Task 1.— Experiment turning the body both forwards and backwards between two ropes.

Task 2.—Swing on one rope, twisting and turning at the end of the action.

Individuals will invent their own methods of using one or two ropes to bring about twisting providing they have understood principles involved.

Apparatus—horse, saddles, box and buck, used singly

Task1—Find ways of getting on and off showing a change of direction.

Task 2.—Get on and find ways of getting off so that the body finishes facing the apparatus.

Task 3.—Get on and jump off and roll, at some point bring about a twist.

When setting out more complicated apparatus it will help if the apparatus is placed initially at angles other than ninety degrees.

Apparatus—form angled to a horse and a mat.

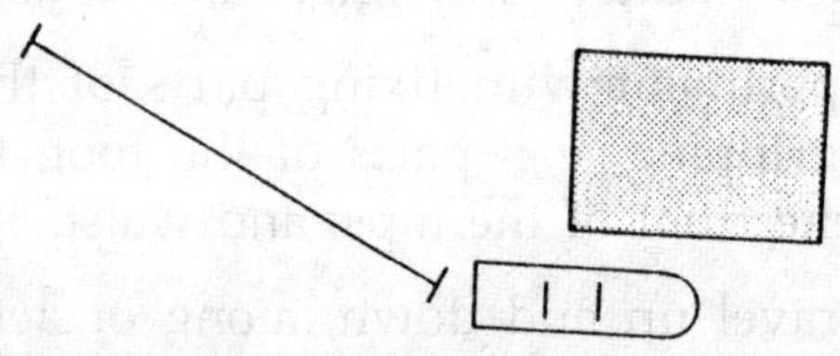

Apparatus—form angled to a box and a mat.

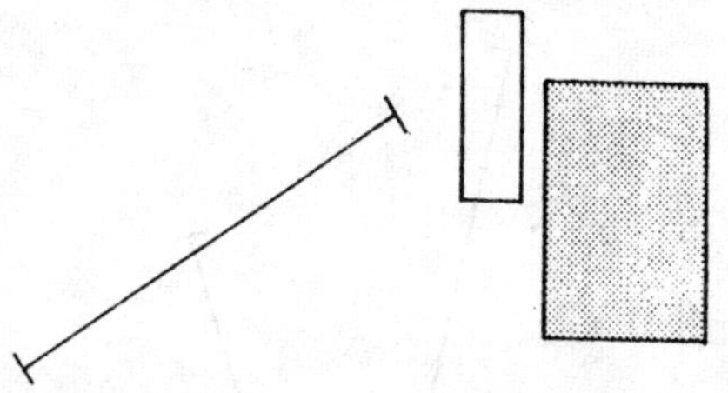

Apparatus-form angled to a bar box, ropes and a mat.

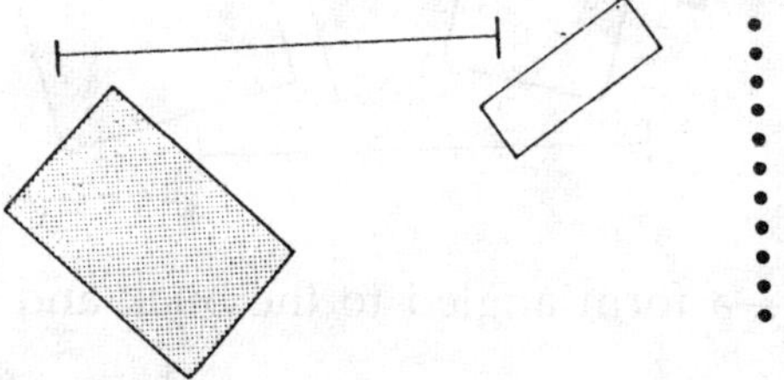

Apparatus—a low bar, one form inclined and one on the floor, two saddles and two mats.

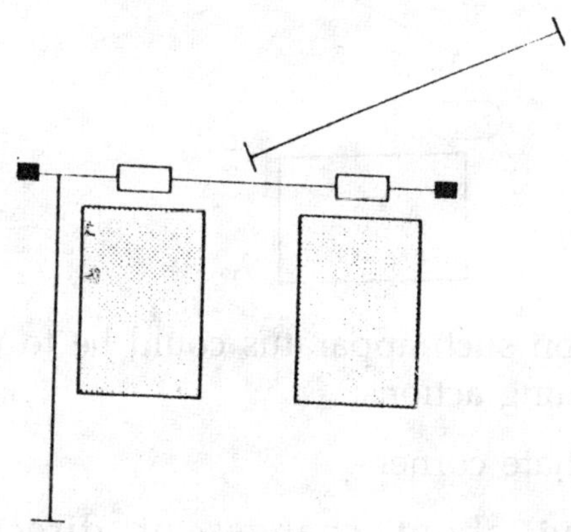

Apparatus—a bar at medium height, three forms, one

underneath the bar, one inclined and one on the floor, two mats.

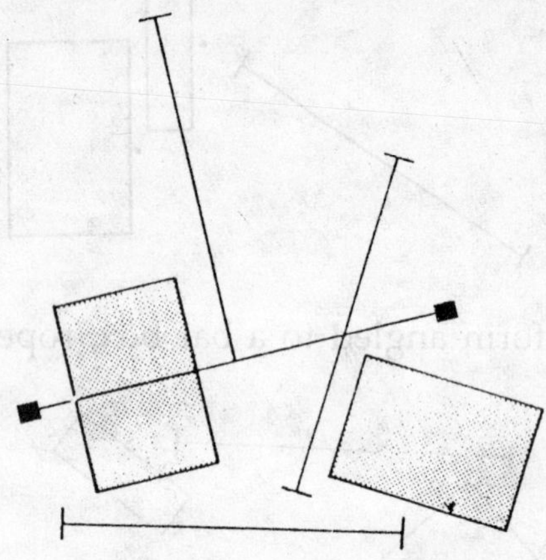

Apparatus—a form angled to the buck and a mat.

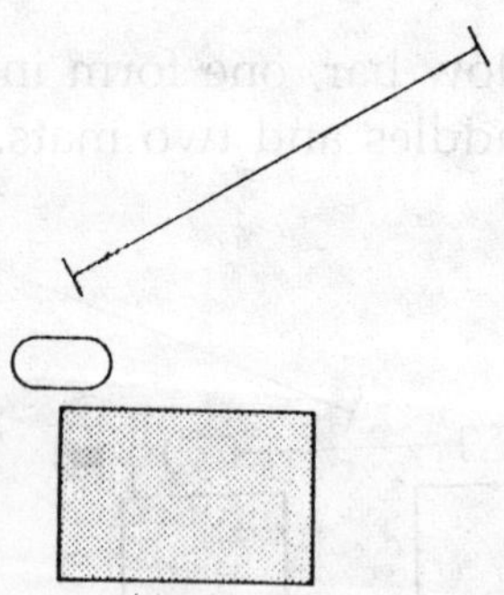

Tasks on such apparatus could be to use twisting and/or turning actions:

(a) to negotiate corners,

(b) to bring about changes of direction while travelling,.

(c) to initiate a change of level.

Symmetry and asymmetry

Symmetry can be defined as equal proportions of the whole being distributed on either side of a line or plane into two or more parts exactly similar in size, shape and position relative to the dividing points. The term bilateral symmetry is used when reference is made to the structure the body; the balance of parts being equal on either side with the limbs arranged matching and in opposition relation to the central dividing line of the vertebral column

Although the body itself is symmetrical, the majority actions are performed asymmetrically. Eating, writing, walking are asymmetrical activities, where one side only'', stressed or where the sides are used alternately. Rarely does one sit, stand or lie symmetrically although unlike writing and walking this is a possibility.

Symmetrical movement in gymnastics demands discipline control, coordination and a keen sense of body awareness. Symmetrical locomotion is limited to the forward-backward direction and movements up and down, as any deviation from these leads into actions with a one-sided stress. In asymmetrical actions one side of the body becomes more active or a greater stress is laid on the right or left. This brings about uneven, lopsided actions where the body has to adapt to unequal and irregular stresses and all manner of twists and turns and changes of direction become possible. Twisting and turning are related to each other and both are associated with asymmetry. Turning about the side to side axis, however, is the only method of rotation where symmetrical or asymmetrical movement is possible. Turning about the up-down and forward-backward axis, where the body is divided into right and left sides will, of necessity, require one side to lead and an asymmetrical action will result.

Experience of both symmetrical and asymmetrical ways of moving are valuable in that each makes a particular demand upon the performer. Moving symmetrically requires skill and an ability to manage the body in a stable, balanced way, where a feeling of precision and poise can be experienced. A greater, variety of action is possible within asymmetrical movements giving the inventive performer an opportunity to experience the one-sided stress and to master completely new skills Jiving uneven distribution of weight..

Teaching

The theme is rather more advanced than those previously taken, so that in the beginning it is dealt with in a very elementary way. Perhaps with young children the words themselves may not even be mentioned, other words such as matching", "balanced", "even", "level", "lopsided", "odd" and "Uneven" can be substituted. It will be found useful, however, to have covered the first stages of this concept before attempting more advanced work, as many progressions depend upon the performer being able to manage his body in both symmetrical and asymmetrical situations and to appreciate the relationship between this idea and twisting and turning, for example, or gaining and terminating balance. Initially each child can experience the symmetry of his own body by standing with weight equally distributed over both feet, appreciating the spine as the dividing line, the head being considered here as an extension of the spine, with the rest of the body matching on either side. Children can the be helped to explore other ways of achieving symmetry using a variety of bases. Within this task the body can be stretched, spread, rounded and arched. Symmetrical ways of travelling will be found and the limitations realised, among them that a double take-off only is possible and that body is restricted to the forward and backward direction and movements up and down. For many this will mean that balances on hands and head, and backward rolls previously achieved with a one-sided stress, must now be mastered in a new way, presenting a challenging situation to the more able.

Asymmetrical use of the body is easier to appreciate on the precision of symmetry has been experienced, the children realising that the former provides a much greater freedom of action. The teacher should be careful here to see that asymmetrical actions are always purposeful. For example ' posing on the shoulders with one leg stretched and the other' bent is of little value, unless either the latter is being prepared, to take weight in a backward movement or the body is going to be brought on to the feet and an asymmetrical placing is required for the following action.

It is essential that children experience the unusual adjustments which have to be made as a result of asymmetric bases. Skilful redistribution of weight above sloping or irregular bases makes new demands even on the more able gymnasts, and it is this aspect which should be emphasised.

Often classes are found experimenting with the asymmetrical placement of limbs above a very stable symmetric base; an undemanding task which makes no reference to the interesting and skilful shifts and adjustments of weight which should be resulting from work on this theme.

Even greater demands can be made if moving both symmetrically and asymmetrically is linked. The skill involved in familiar actions such as handstands and cart-wheels can be extended by introducing such ideas as following:

(a) lead into and out of a handstand asymmetrically but achieve symmetry at the point of balance;

(b) lead into a handstand symmetrically and resolve asymmetrically;

(c) perform the whole action symmetrically;

(d) interrupt a cartwheel midway and achieve symmetry either complete the action normally or maintain symmetry to land.

This theme is valuable in that clarity, precision and a heightened sense of body awareness are required and, although some will find symmetrical actions difficult to master, the discipline and control demanded lead both to improved skill and to a more discriminating appreciation of line.

Apparatus

In Olympic gymnastics many of the vaults are symmetrical, necessitating double takeoffs and two-foot landings. The apparatus itself is usually placed symmetrically and in most cases body follows a straight line in a forward direction.

In sequential work, however, a blending of symmetry and asymmetry is encouraged to produce added variety and a more skilful use of the body when moving over apparatus.

Symmetrical actions on apparatus, as on the floor, are limited number but require added control, balance and body awareness when working at the different levels provided by the apparatus. The possibilities of producing asymmetrical actions are greatly increased once apparatus is introduced as the variations in height of gripping surfaces can be exploited.

In the first few lessons on this theme with beginners it will be sufficient for the children to appreciate that the hands and feet can be used symmetrically and asymmetrically and they can experiment with ways of travelling along, up and down and over apparatus using one foot or two feet, one hand or two hands and also explore the possibilities of combining the symmetrical use of hands and asymmetrical use of feet, and vice versa. The task of travelling using two hands and two feet symmetrically along a form will probably but not necessarily result in the rest of the body moving symmetrically. In such cases the teacher could point out that in these actions not only do the limbs work symmetrically but the whole body travels with both sides matching. The class can then be given various pieces of apparatus to use such as climbing frames, ladders, planks, forms, steps, low box to or stage blocks and challenged to travel symmetrically.

This method of moving on apparatus may be restricting juniors and so should not be pursued for long. The majority will probably grasp the main idea quite quickly and show, both symmetrical and asymmetrical ways of travelling.

Provided that adequate time has been allowed for exploration at floor level the work on apparatus can progress very quickly at a later stage. Tasks on forms can be given which will guide the class towards appreciating that an asymmetrical, base is inevitable when using the two levels.

Apparatus—form used broadside uppermost.

Task 1.—Travel along placing the hands symmetrically the form.

Task 2.—Travel across and back again using hands symmetrically on the form.

Task 3.—Travel along and across using alternate hands to take weight.

Task 4.—Travel along or across placing hands asymmetrically.

Task 5.—Travel along or across placing one hand on the form and one on the floor.

Rolling symmetrically along forms forwards and back wards can be attempted. In some cases it will be found easier to achieve symmetry rolling along forms than on the floor particularly if the feet and the trunk are at different levels.

Apparatus—form narrow side uppermost.

Apparatus—mats.

Task 1—Cross the mat symmetrically and recross a metrically.

Task 2.—Work out an asymmetrical balance sequence.

Task 3.—Travel around the edge of the mat using

symmetrical movements, progress forwards and backwards, negotiate the corners asymmetrically.

Task 4. —Approach the mat, cross and move away with matching and asymmetrical actions.

Apparatus—forms and mats.

Task 1— Use both pieces of apparatus, showing symmetrical movements on one, asymmetrical on the other.

Task 2,—Using the form and mat together, achieve asymmetrical balance positions.

Task 3.—Jump over the form or use it to gain height. Gain symmetrical and asymmetrical body shapes in the air.

Apparatus—bar, hip height.

Task 1—,Cross the bar asymmetrically, recross symmetrically.

Task 2—,Cross asymmetrically, get under symmetrically.

Task 3 — Travel from one end to the other with asymmetrical movements on the bar and symmetrical move on the floor.

Apparatus—double bars, low and medium height.

Task 1— Travel up, over and down with a one-sided stress.

Task 2— Use one bar to show symmetrical actions and the other asymmetrical actions.

Task 3—Travel along using both bars together with a one sided stress; develop a rhythmical phrasing.

Apparatus— climbing frames.

Task 1—Travel up showing symmetrical movements, *through* and down with asymmetrical movements.

Task 2.—Invent a sequence travelling symmetrically and asymmetrically alternately.

When planning apparatus the placement can do much to suggest the appropriate use of symmetrical or asymmetrical actions. Apparatus set in a straight line will probably lead to a predominance of symmetrical movements, particularly if the task is to keep on the apparatus. Skilled performers Might, however, easily produce a completely asymmetrical sequence. Apparatus placed at a variety of angles and offering different levels will help the beginner to travel asymmetrically.

Apparatus—a low box with four mats.

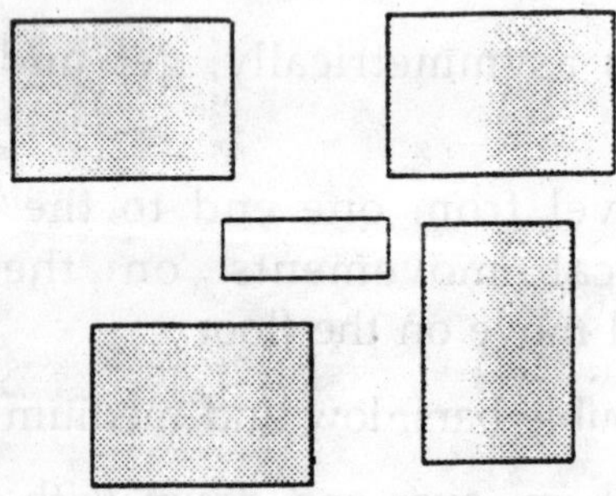

Task.—Arrive from a variety of angles, change direction to get off. Get on and off taking weight on hands stressing symmetrical and asymmetrical use of hands and feet.

Apparatus—two forms leading up to saddles on a low

bar an two mats. The apparatus is duplicated so that six or more children can be divided into two groups.

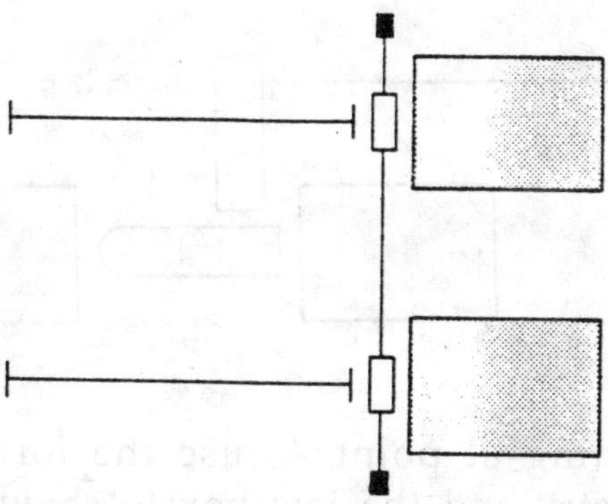

Task.—Using all the apparatus, including a return activity over the bar. Stress symmetry but achieve asymmetry at least once.

Apparatus—a set of ropes, mattress and two forms.

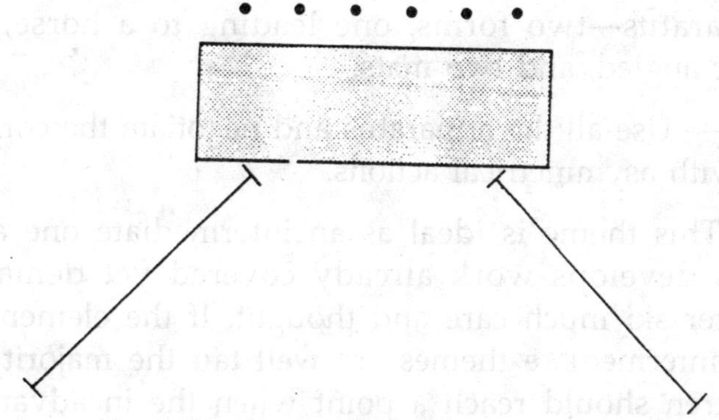

Task—Take any starting point and, using all the apparatus, stress asymmetry.

Apparatus–a form leading to a low box, a horse and two mats.

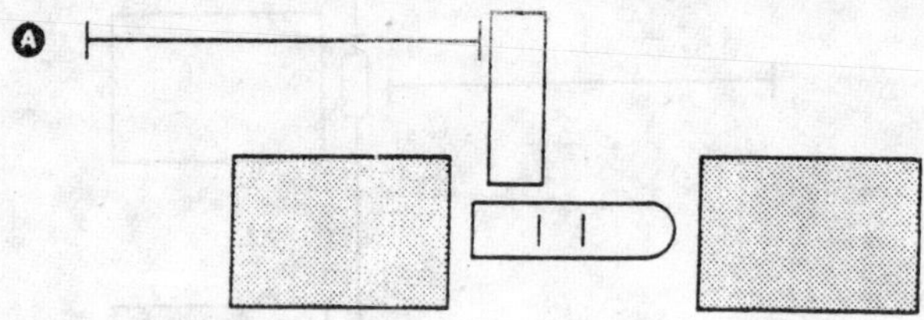

Task—Starting at point A, use the form to show asymmetry and the low box to show symmetry move either symmetrically or asymmetrically over the horse.

Apparatus—four ropes and a box

Task.—Use assisted flight on to the box from any angle, transfer weight and achieve flight off the box.

Apparatus—two forms, one leading to a horse, the other angled, and two mats.

Task.— Use all the apparatus and negotiate the corners with asymmetrical actions.

This theme is ideal as an intermediate one as it links develops work already covered yet demands greater ski much care and thought. If the elementary and intermediate themes are well tau the majority of children should reach a point when the in advanced work can be approached with confidence. It should be stressed that the early stages us' thoroughly explored and sufficient time given to each idea so that interest, enjoyment, satisfaction, confidence skill are all experienced before presenting the advanced themes.

4

CONTROL OF BODY WEIGHT

Skilful control is one of the most important aims in gymnastics. In order to achieve physical mastery the child must learn to manage his body weight and to produce the appropriate of tension and energy required in a variety of actions. It is necessary to define some of the terms used in describing the body and the way in which it acts. The *kinesthetic sense is* the means by which changing muscular *tensions* are felt. The *weight* of the body is measurable and subject to the laws of gravity. The body produces *energy* which is the driving force for movement. All movement involves degree of resistance, whether this is produced within the body itself or from without by people or by apparatus. Resistance is overcome by using measurable degree of *strength.*

Control of weight

The control of body weight is one of the first considerations in gymnastics. The terms "weight bearing", "taking weight", "changing weight" and "transfering weight" suggest different movement considerations but they have in common the necessity to become aware of and manage the weight. Since the body is subject to gravity it is usually necessary to resist this and resulting actions range from maintaining an upright position to actually ejecting the body into the air. An awareness of the pelvic region, where the centre of gravity is normally located, is vital in all situations where weight is being controlled.

Even in comparatively simple actions such as transferring weight from one base to another, management is Import particularly when the bases are far apart. The body weight must be held over the original base until it can be transfer onto the new base, otherwise falling or collapsing m result. Control in such situations can also be achieved by trunk and free limbs leaning or pulling away from the that is to bear weight, counteracting the tendency to topple over, until the new base is ready. In balancing actions free limbs can be used to make fine adjustments so that weight is controlled and retained over the base.

In actions such as swinging the weight is instrumental bringing about change, impetus being gained and recharged" by an active use of the body weight. Similarly, balance can terminated by deliberately moving the centre of gravity that it falls outside the base.

When a certain degree of control is attained and the body weight can be guided safely and used effectively, it is pro able to experiment with tipping, tilting or leaning action' In these situations the weight can be shifted gradually that, in order to avoid falling, locomotion takes place. If the weight is "let go" and caught again its role in stability and mobility can be recognised and exploited.

It is more difficult to control weight in the three phases flight, that is, at takeoff, while the body is in the air, a when it meets the floor again, than in situations where,,, contact with the floor or apparatus is maintained.

Control of tension and energy

When muscular tension is present the body is active whether it is moving or holding a position. Lack of tension results in heaviness. The latter state taken to its extreme is the antithesis of movement and bodily control. Increasing tension produces gripping in the whole or parts of the body while decreasing tension leads to relaxing. In all gymnastic actions muscular tension is present some it is particularly important. When balancing the is kept over the base and this implies that a certain degree of tension is produced. In holding a balanced position the body should have sufficient tension to maintain an upward stress rather than give way to a weighty, downward one. Actions concerned with a poised arrival on apparatus, especially from flight, involve changing degrees of tension. This enables the Movement through space to be arrested and the body to achieve stillness, so that a balance can be maintained.

In gymnastics the floor provides the resistance against which the body pushes in order to lift or jump and to which the body adapts on landing. In apparatus work where obstacles have to be mounted or cleared the energy expended is often considerable. For any type of jump to be effective there must be an outburst of energy. Similarly the release of a full twist, the slashing action of' the legs to turn the body when swinging on a rope, the whipping action of the free limbs to cause loss of balance, the pressing of the hands against the floor or apparatus during inversion, are all characterised by the strength required or efficient performance. Actions requiring less output of energy generally occur when the body is poised on apparatus, in some pinpoint balances, and while the body is the air.

The body must be involved as a unit when producing energy whether the result is manifest in actions of the whole body an isolated part. Because the hips are associated with the, centre of gravity it is essential that the lower half of the body, is used to maximum effect when strong actions are required. The upper half of the body, particularly the head and chest, become important in actions where the energy output is reduced.

An awareness of the changing tensions and the differing amounts of energy which the body can produce is vital to the gymnast. Without this awareness the work might be bodily competent but lacking in quality, vitality and interest. Indeed, one hallmark of a very able gymnast is the ability to make actions demanding much skill and energy appear effortless. This illusory aspect as when, for example, a skilled performer is seen to soar through the air to alight in a perfect inverted balance on high apparatus without any obvious output of energy would, it seems, qualify the act to worthy of aesthetic consideration.

In gymnastics there is a certain association between rate at which the body moves and the amount of energy expended. The most usual combination is seen in strong quick actions. Inverting the body, getting off the ground and on to or over high apparatus usually necessitates a strong action which, in order to be effective, must be executed quickly. This combination of speed and energy gives to gymnastics its characteristic zest.

All movement involves body weight and, to a greater lesser degree, tension and energy. Therefore, this is not theme to be taken over a series of lessons but should be ever-present consideration of the teacher who leads the children progressively towards an understanding of the problems involved. The relevant aspects of weight, tension and energy are discussed in each specific theme but it is profitable to see how the teacher can develop these throughout the work as a whole. In the elementary stages children are given varied experiences which are aimed at enlivening their kinesthetic sense The awareness and control of the body weight is an intrinsic' part of this fundamental work. Locomotion, stillness, weight bearing and weight transference are situations in which management of weight is the prime concern. Children physical growth should always be taken into account; height weight and proportions alter, so the teacher cannot expect that once control is gained at any particular stage it remain. Because of this and the fact that new situations presented as the work progresses, control of weight is an aspect of movement to which the teacher should refer frequently.

In curling, stretching, twisting and turning, children feel the different tensions which are characteristic of actions. The weaker tension and inward focus of curling should be contrasted with the two-way outward pull stretching, the radiating tensions of spreading and the vary stretched and compressed tensions within twisting. The teacher must ensure that children experience these tensions often, and to the full, for the particular tensional "feel" associated with an action should be remembered and retained, so that it becomes a part of the movement experience that can be reproduced accurately when required. Symmetry asymmetry and body shape in stillness and when moving are also achieved by muscular tensions and the bodily "feel" is again important. When children can consider and control the changing tensions within their bodies their work bccomes livelier and clarity of movement is possible.

Although output of energy has always to be considered in gymnastics the first time this is stressed is probably when flight introduced as a way of transferring weight. In all jumping activities, particularly in bouncing, where resilient recoveries are important, considerable energy is needed. With children, whose energy seems limitless in this respect teacher has an excellent opportunity to make certain that these activities are fully experienced so that they can be extended and built upon later.

In order to tackle the more advanced themes children must have acquired a degree of bodily mastery which includes Control of weight and the ability to select appropriate and output of energy. Management of weight and control of tension is necessary in moving slowly and in addition quick actions demand much energy. In helping children achieve continuity of action the teacher must realise that it is only when weight, tension and energy can be controlled and used effectively that a blending of adjacent actions becomes possible.

When children work with a partner or within a group they are often in a situation where they have to cope with the weight of others, and this entails producing comparatively great degrees of strength. In the advanced themes of balance or flight the teacher should appreciate that the former is more concerned with weight and tension while in the latter it is the energy involved that is stressed.

The resistance and firm base provided by the asphalt Playground and the wooden floor are accepted but rarely used in a conscious manner. Just as apparatus can be considered as an extension of the floor, in this respect the floor should be used as a piece of apparatus. One way of developing sensitivity is to set "touch before contact tasks. In these the body part about to receive weight briefly touches the floor or apparatus prior to being placed ready for weight bearing. Such tasks need not be pursued for an, length of time since their purpose is to aid sensitivity they are not an end in themselves.

The one type of apparatus in which the control of body weight, tension and energy is of prime importance is aiding the "take-off" phase of flight. Beating boards, spring boards and trampettes all require considerable skill in the use if they are to be effective.

5

THE USE OF SPACE

The individual's interest in space is twofold. Firstly, his attention can be focussed on the space immediately surrounding the body, which is within his reach by normal on the extension. Secondly, the space shared by others and confined only by the walls of the gymnasium or playground or broken and sectioned by apparatus, can be equally important.

In the following aspects of this theme the focus of attention is on *where* the body is moving. In gymnastics movement follows either a straight or roundabout *pathway,* and at any time during locomotion, the body can be moving in one of three di*rections* and at one of three *levels.* The *shape of the body* in space is constantly changing and this can be considered in both locomotion and stillness.

Pathways

Locomotion is one of the main concerns in gymnastics and although the first consideration is body stressed, the track made when travelling is inextricably linked. At floor level, pathways involving the general space are immediately dictated by obstacles in the way of the mover. These may be mobile or stationary; mobile in the case of others also working in the general space, stationary when the deviations in track necessitated by walls, railings, projections or apparatus are considered. While travelling the body can move in a straight line, along straight lines producing angular floor patterns, or can swerve and twist following a circuitous route. The relation between straight pathways and the symmetrical use of the body can be appreciated as well as the connection between twisting, asymmetry and the resulting indirect tracks. The course followed over apparatus can also vary with special attention being paid to angles of approaching and leaving the apparatus.

The floor and air patterns resulting from travelling actions will usually be incidental, but a growing awareness and ability to move fluently should be stimulated, and the deliberate following of a variety of pathways encouraged.

Direction

When considering direction the attention is focused on the space immediately surrounding the body into which a part or the whole is about to move. The main directions in which the body travels in gymnastics are forwards, backwards and sideways and these are closely linked with stability. Deliberately moving into a diagonal direction can be associated with certain aspects of flight and loss of balance where momentary instability is experienced. A change of direction can be brought about in two ways. The body can move forward, backward and then sideways,

(a) with no change of front, ot

(b) continuing along a straight path, each action linked by a turn or twist.

When studying the relationship between twisting, turning, symmetry, asymmetry and change of direction, certain links' can be established.

Symmetrical travelling is limited to the *forward* and *back,,, ward* directions, while moving *asymmetrically* allows the body to perform actions in all directions including those to the *side* and along the *diagonal.*

Twisting brings about continuous *changes of direction. Turning* about the *vertical axis* allows a *change of front* occur. *Turning* about the *side to side axis* limits the moment to a *forward and backward direction. Turning* about the *forward and backward axis* brings about actions to *side.*

Level

When changes of level are observed it is the body as whole which must be studied. Actions which elevate take the body *high* into the space beyond the normal reach, while those which keep the body moving near the floor involve travelling at the low level. The *medium* level in gymnastics tends to be "moved through" rather than stressed.

Body shape

The shape the body makes while travelling or in stillness is, at times, incidental. An awarenesss of the body outline in space and consequent shape, however, can often help clarify actions.

When curling, stretching, arching and twisting occur it is actions that are stressed, the shape of the body remaining of secondary importance. Once the action becomes part of movement vocabulary, a progression can be recognised the shape of the body assumes a greater importance the attention of the performer can be directed towards body contour. It is here that the arch achieved in a back bend can be fully appreciated, the wide, extended star shape of the cartwheel more defined and the elongation of the h,: in a handstand perfected. This is the stage when definition of shape adds clarity of line to an action and a positive attitude towards the body shape in space can be adopted. It may well be that the noticeable increase in the number of girls wearing gymnastic leotards has had a significant influence on awareness of body outline and consciousness of alignment.

The difference between movements where the body shape is maintained throughout the action, as in cartwheels and rolls, and those where a specific shape is only momentarily achieved, as in a handstand, can be contrasted. The shapes that the body can assume while airborne can be explored. It has already been stated that stretching is simpler than tucking, but both are possible. Twisting and turning where changes of direction and front occur can also be achieved if anticipated in the take-off.

Apparatus limits the space and provides barriers to get over, under, in and out, through and round. In manoeuvring the body the shape is constantly changing, always adapting the new situations presented by the apparatus. Moving partners and mobile apparatus such as ropes can provide both novel and challenging situations in that the fine timing required to negotiate spaces which are continuously alter demands considerable skill.

These themes are essential if children are to appreciate and become aware of themselves in relation to others or apparatus. It is also important if they are to become adept at judging heights and distances relative to tne body. In both cases it can be seen as a vital safety factor when children are moving in the gymnasium or playground. The awareness of both personal and general space is necessary if these are to be exploited, variety achieved and the body used to its fullest extent.

Pathways

When travelling on feet the natural reaction of young children is to move around the hall or playground following a circular track and moving in a forward direction. If, however, they begin facing one other person they can be give," the task of running, dodging and swerving to avoid others. This starting position is one way of ensuring that individuals will be facing different directions and when travelling commences an avoiding action must immediately be take When other tasks have been answered involving locomotion often a greater variety can be achieved if the attention drawn to the floor patterns created. The teacher may diet the track or the class may be left free to invent their own The following patterns are but a few from which a selection can be made.

Young children enjoy the challenge of producing recognisable floor patterns while travelling. It should be noted direction and level of work are unimportant at this stage, it is the pathway that is stressed.

Suggested tasks linking locomotion and track:

Task 1 Travel on hands and feet making a zig-zag path.

Task 2 Travel on parts of the trunk creating a curved pathway

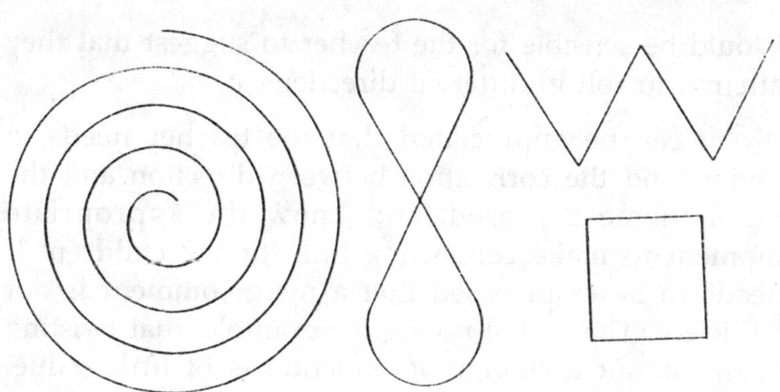

Task 3 Roll, making a circular track on the floor.

Older children could also work on this idea but it would not be necessary to dwell on pathways at floor level. The teacher could draw attention to the possibilities and refer incidentally to this when dealing with later themes and when working on apparatus. Air tracks could be explored with some classes, stressing the long, low trajectory required for length or the high, curving course needed if height is to be gained. Twists and turns while the body is upright in flight can be experienced by all, while actions where the body rotates in the air about other axes can be attempted by the few.

Direction

This aspect of space has an obvious link with the elementary body management themes and can be considered at any stage, when the main idea has been grasped. If, for example, a class has mastered travelling and stopping or pausing, an added challenge might be to change direction after each Interruption. When children have experimented with rolling actions, it

Would be sensible for the teacher to suggest that they attempt to roll in different directions.

It can be appreciated that the teacher needs to understand the correlation between direction and the main theme explored, and know the appropriate moment to make connecting link for the children. It needs to be emphasised that a mere comment is not sufficient. The verbal noting for example, that twisting brings about a change of direction is of little value. This point must be translated into action and the children allowed time to explore the idea anew, this knowledge adding to their awareness of the movement possibilities.

The following tasks are examples of how the link can made between directional changes and other themes.

Task 1.Starting on the feet, transfer the weight onto shoulders. Find three ways of answering this task showing movement into different directions.

Task 2. Invent a sequence which includes stretching arching and curling-each action must lead the body into a different direction.

Task 3.—Using a variety of bases choose three action which take the feet into the air. Bring about a change of direction by turning or twisting.

Task 4.—Run, jump and turn in the air a backward or sideways roll results.

Level

Locomotion necessarily involves the body moving at on level or another, but when exploring this idea the stress is mainly on extending the normal range; getting as high or low as possible and experiencing the transitions when moving, easily through all three. Young children enjoy pulling and pushing themselves along the floor, slithering and sliding, keeping very near to ground. They delight in leaping and throwing themselves to the floor or launching themselves into space. They re space and need a sufficient area to experience this freedom.

Older children in general seem less inclined to exploit the space; few experience the exhilaration of true flight enjoy moving very near to the ground. The three phases of flight must therefore at this stage be handled carefully, and particular attention given landings and efficient takeoffs if confidence which may have been lost or undermined is to be restored. It is essential that children move fluently and without restraint at any level, and tasks involving leaping and rolling, including turning in the air and change of direction, springing on to the hands and dive rolls should be given. The teacher must help children to move confidently from one level to another on the floor or forms before expecting work on this idea to be attempted on higher apparatus.

Body shape

The concern or die teacher should be to ensure that the facility with which actions are performed is such that the attention is no longer devoted entirely to the skill but can be directed also towards the shape of the body as it moves in space.

Attention can be drawn to body shape in a held position and clarity demanded

(a) at the beginning and end of a sequence,

(b) in a held balance, or

(c) by the individual providing an obstacle for a partner.

With older, more experienced classes, the teacher can expect a heightened awareness of the body in motion, on floor level, and in flight. The changing body shapes in tucked jumps or catsprings, for example, can do much not only to clarify the action but also to help the performer master the skill. Shape can readily be appreciated through observation of others and the teacher should take advantage of this by including short sessions in the introductory stages. Thus what is meant by shape can be seen, understood and implemented in the child's own work.

Pathways

Pathways over apparatus are at first incidental to the actions performed but tracks become increasingly important as variety of approach and inventive use of apparatus are stressed. Pathways can be influenced by the arrangement apparatus—the two examples below suggesting the obvious but not necessarily the only, pathway.

It should be noted that placement of spring boards, forms and mats particularly, does much to influence starting finishing points.

A variety of track can be dictated by the teacher in,", task set, although the placement of apparatus, as in following example, suggests a straight line pathway.

Apparatus—form, low box, horse and mat.

Task— Travel over the apparatus making a zig-zag track.

A number of tracks should be possible in an arrangement so that individuals may choose their own, but the groups should be kept small so that, if desired, all may work at once. One example is given below of such an apparatus arrangement.

Apparatus— ropes, two bars, one form inclined to the high bar the other flat, a spring board, box and horse.

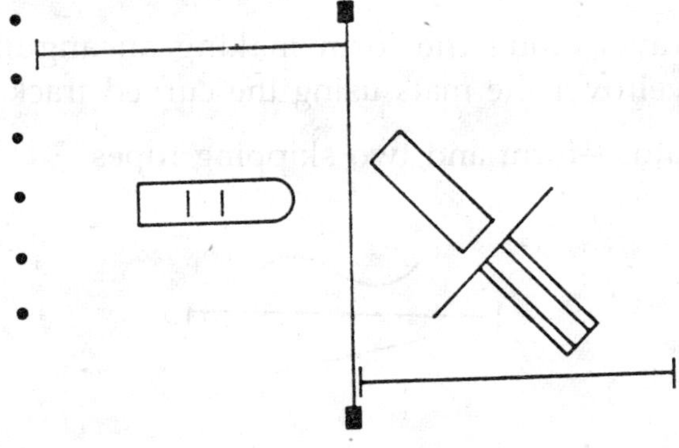

When stressing pathways attention should be drawn to spaces between apparatus and to the use of the floor in linking actions. If this point is not appreciated the continuity of action over apparatus is often interrupted and disjointed. At an early stage children should be encouraged to use floor space. Return activities utilising the floor can be suggested if apparatus is limited, e.g. when forms only are provided the challenge might include a floor task. With younger classes small apparatus placed on the ground h to direct attention to possible paths, as in the following examples.

Apparatus—a form and four individual mats.

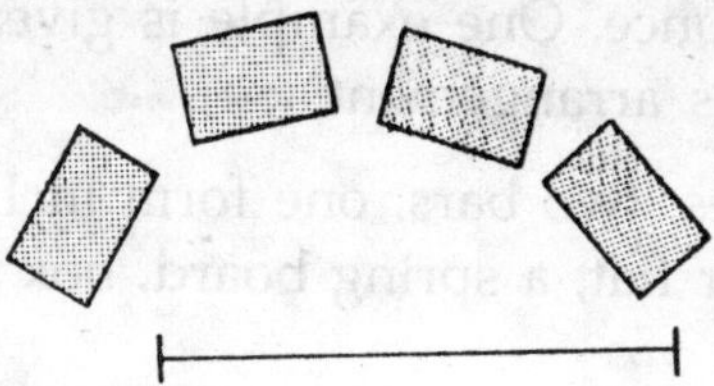

*Task.*Travel along the form making an angular path travel over the mats using the curved track.

Apparatus—form and two skipping ropes.

*Task.*Travel along the form and return using either rope showing a clear change of path.

The air tracks can be highlighted when clearing apparatus by repetitive actions involving flight for example:

Apparatus—three forms placed at regular intervals and broadways.

Task.—Run and jump over or on and off each form producing repetitive air patterns.

A variation of this task could be to provide a situation both height and length are included.

Apparatus—two layers of the box leading to a high bar.

Task. Run and use the box to leap on to the bar, swing and drop to the floor.

Air tracks can be stressed when swinging on ropes, where the pathway the body makes through the air can vary. If the body is, taken into the air and released from the rope at the highest point, the air pattern is different from that made by the body if it swings into the air and is released only when the feet touch the floor at the lowest part of the swing.

Once this aspect of space has been dealt with it can be referred to whatever the main theme of the lesson. The teacher can, expect the class to become increasingly aware of the variety of pathways possible on apparatus, and to select specific tracks relevant to the situation.

Direction

The most natural way of travelling on apparatus is to move forwards this must be taken into account when setting tasks which dictate direction. Apparatus which has to be mounted or cleared must of necessity be approached with the body moving forwards, but once in contact with the apparatus a change of direction can take place. Leaving the apparatus can equally well be effected moving backwards or sideways.

Apparatus such as bars, ropes and window ladders provide ample opportunity for moving in any direction, including the diagonal.

Flight into different directions can be experienced from forms, spring boards and trampettes and with the more skilled classes flight into the diagonal can be attempted.

Tasks on apparatus can ensure that the beginner experiences moving in to all directions.

Apparatus—three mats

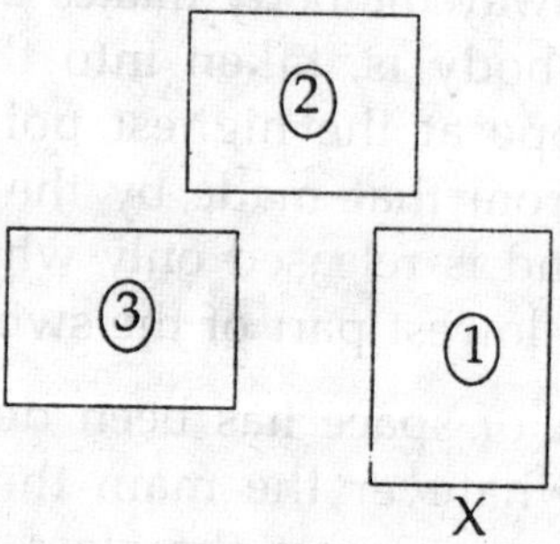

Task.—With X as the starting point, work over all mats, forwards over mat 1, sideways over mat 2 backwards over mat 3

Apparatus—a form and mat.

Task.—Begin facing the form at X — cross and recross form travelling forwards and backwards; move sideways over the mat.

Apparatus— box top, mat and form

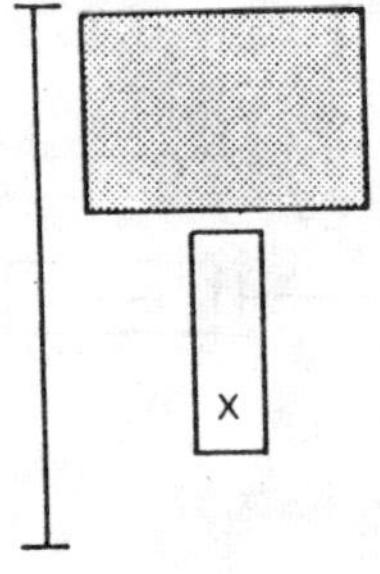

Task. Starting at X move backwards over the box, ways across the mat and forwards along the form.

Apparatus—spring board or trampette and mats.

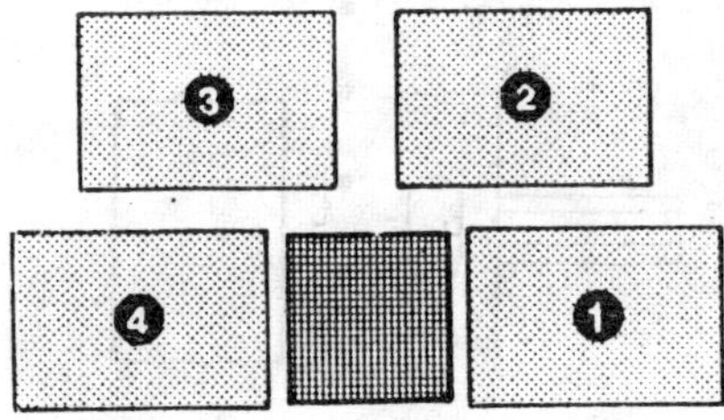

Task: Using the spring board or trampette, run, jump and land, At the first attempt land on mat 1 and from subsequent jumps land on 2, 3 and 4 in turn.

When children have explored the various possibilities of moving in different directions much more freedom can be given, for example:

Apparatus—high and low bar.

Task Using each bar separately and at one point together *include* three changes of direction.

Apparatus—form, box, ropes and mattress.

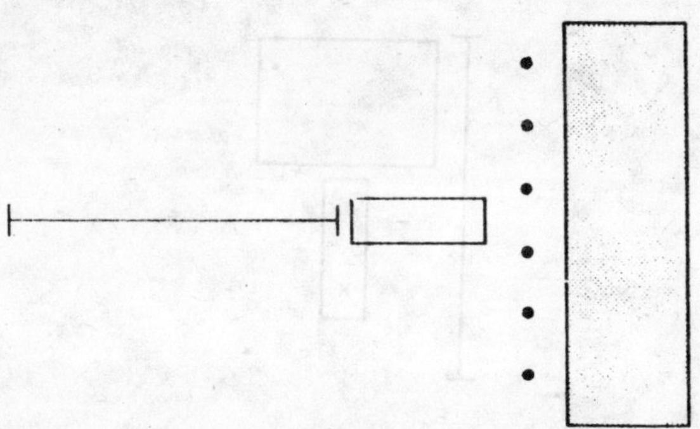

Task—Start at the end of the form and travel to the mattress changing direction twice.

Apparatus—spring board, buck, ropes and mat.

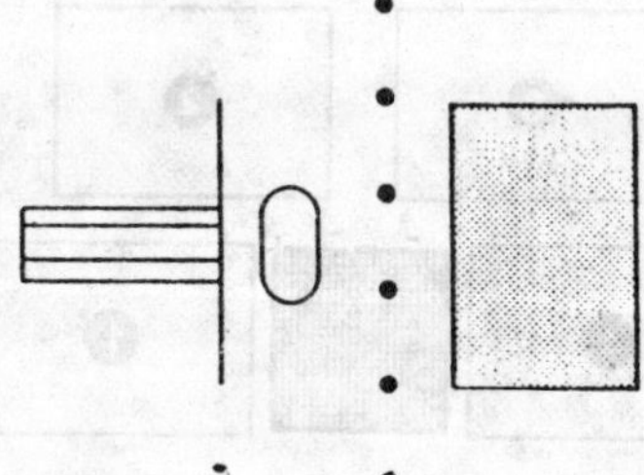

Task. While travelling, bring about changes of direction by twisting and turning.

Level

When apparatus is introduced, level becomes a dual, consideration; the level on which the body is moving relative to the apparatus, and the height of the apparatus itself. Working in contact with apparatus which is at a height from the floor does not mean that the body is moving in the high area, although a feeling of being high may well be experienced.

Taking the body into the high level can be achieved by leaping onto, off or over steps, stage blocks, low tables box tops, forms, spring boards and trampettes. Incline forms or planks to stools, bar box or bar can be used on the class has the confidence to exploit these situations. Flight is more readily experienced leaving apparatus than when arriving but, if the task involves jumping from too great, a height too soon, flight off may be inhibited since anticipation of landing will occur and rather than reaching into the space above the action will become one of dropping.

The ability to land resiliently from a height should be encouraged and the skill involved in moving easily from that position either into a roll or to rebound should be mastered.

In the following examples of tasks, the level is dictated but whenever apparatus is being planned the teacher should keep in mind that level is an important factor.

Apparatus-hoop held parallel to the ground by a partner or a cane raised on skittles.

Task. Run and leap high into or over the hoop or over cane and return low by sliding or rolling underneath.

Apparatus—individual mats.

Task Run and jump high over the mat, return keeping near to the ground.

Apparatus—form.

Task. Cross and recross alternately using the form to gain height and to keep low

Apparatus—form and mats

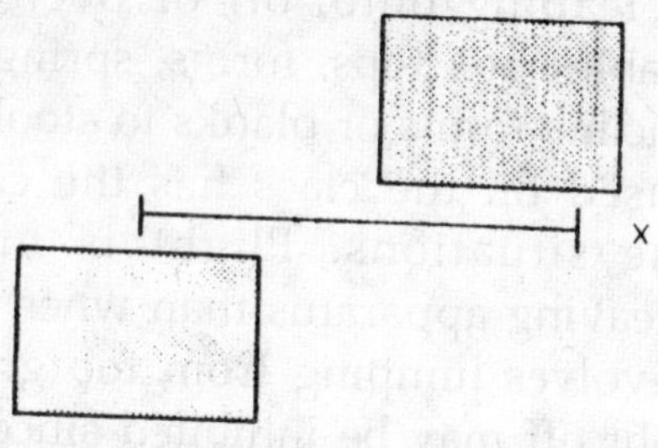

Task. Starting at X, move over the form and mats emphasising medium and low levels.

Apparatus—bar and mats height of bar to be determined by the height and ability of the group.

Task—Run and leap to grip the bar, land and roll across the mat.

Apparatus—inclined form on to a low bar and mat.

Task— Run and jump off the form, roll across the mat and return over the bar keeping the body near to the apparatus

Apparatus trampette, trapeze, high bar and mattress.

Task— Show changes of level while travelling over the apparatus.

Apparatus—two layers of the box, trampette, ropes and mattress.

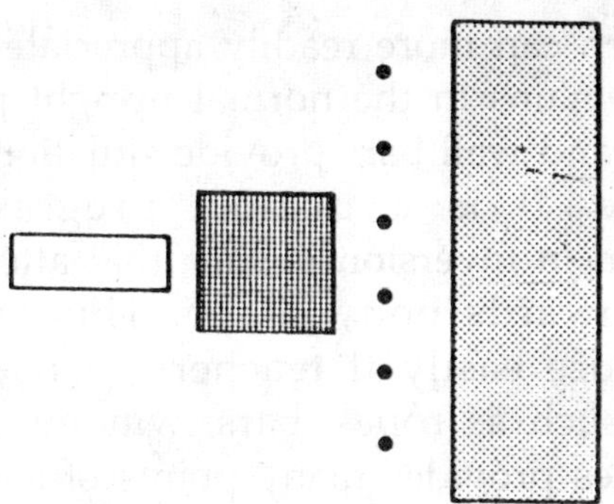

Task. As above.

This arrangement offers greater scope for the more skilled performer since, unlike the previous example, it demands that the gymnast adapts to fluctuations in level. It can also be made progressively more difficult by

(a) raising the box,

(b) increasing the distances between box and trampette and trampette and ropes,

(c) encouraging diagonal flight from the trampette the ropes not immediately ahead.

Body shape

This has to be taught with understanding otherwise static "poses" appear with the held shape bearing no relation to the arrival or method of leaving the apparatus. As in floor work the shape of the body can be considered in stillness or while', travelling. Unlike work at ground level, however, the shape of the body is often dictated by the outline of the apparatus, itself and by the spaces presented.

Children can more readily appreciate shape when the body remains in the normal upright position, and ropes, bars and wall bars provide situations where this is possible. It is a distinct progression when reorientation in inversion is such that attention can be directed towards body shape. This stage can be reached more easily if teachers realise that some apparatus such as ropes, bars, window ladders and parallel ropes provides many points of support. These offer opportunities for the body to be held in or moved into inverted position, affording a degree of security not always experienced on portable apparatus.

When balancing on apparatus has been mastered teacher could turn the attention of the more able children the held shape. This not only provides a further challenge but also helps the performer achieve a greater clarity of movement resulting in more finished work.

Apparatus which assists takeoff allows the performer greater time in the air to achieve, establish and feel body positions. Ropes and bars are ideal apparatus upon which changing body shapes can be experienced while travelling

A more advanced stage is reached when the performer is so competent while moving on and clearing apparatus that awareness of body line can be noted and appreciated.

Much of this work is for the skilled performer and those who are more spatially conscious than others although talented young children, particularly girls, are very capable of producing work which shows an acute and accurate appreciation of body alignment. Boys on the other hand are usually much more interested in acquiring skill; body line and finished work is often neglected, but for the advanced gymnast work on this could produce a much higher standard of performance. No specific tasks or arrangements of apparatus are given as this idea can develop from work already being produced on other themes such as weight bearing, balance or flight.

6

TUMBLING

Tumbling is a basic motor skill that covers extensively the mechanics of rolling, turning, springing, and twisting. From watching children at play, one can see that it is a natural activity to include in a physical education program. Besides the aspect of fun, it serves as a fine background for apparatus work and also as a carry-over activity for other sports. It is challenging and exciting to develop tumbling skills, whether they are elementary or advanced. Tumbling is generally done on tumbling mats in a gymnasium, but there is no reason to avoid performing stunts outdoors on a suitable area of grass or beach.

Mats are available in several different sizes. The more common sizes are 4' x 8', 5' x 10', and 6' x 12' and range in thickness from 1 to 3 inches depending on the type of material used. There are also a variety of landing pads from 4 to 12 inches in thickness. Many instructors prefer the 6-foot width because it provides more space for working across the mats. Longer mats or a series of mats offer the opportunity to perform combinations of stunts, which increases the variety and difficulty of a tumbling program. Some mats are panelled, which allows them to be folded for ease of carrying and storage.

Values

The specific values of tumbling activities are:

1. Tumbling develops coordination and timing.
2. Tumbling develops agility and flexibility because of the nature of the movements involved, Much bending, tucking, and twisting is required to perform the stunts well.
3. Because of the running and springing necessary in tumbling activities, strength is developed in the legs. This is somewhat unique in that most other gymnastic activities tend to neglect the legs.
4. Courage and determination are developed in some of the more daring and difficult tumbling stunts, More advanced stunts involve movements performed with the body completely in the air.
5. Learning to control the body in basic tumbling skills has great carry-over to the other sports.
6. The art of falling correctly, as learned in tumbling, is of great importance in many sports as well as in normal daily activities. A relaxed rolling fall often prevents or reduces injury and enables a person to regain his feet in quickly after a fall.
7. Because tumbling is a natural activity, it is self-motivating and provides a great deal of fun and enjoyment for its participants.

Organization

Area and equipment

Beginning tumbling can be taught in a small area. However, when more advanced stunts are taught or combinations of stunts are put into routines, a run is helpful to build up momentum. Tumbling is best taught using mats. The mats can be put in a small area if used by a squad only or they can be put end to end in a row for mass instruction. For a large class, more than one row of mats may be required. In order for the instructor to see all of the pupils and for the pupils to see the demonstration, a horseshoe pattern would be advantageous. A circle formation is also possible, but it doesn't enable the instructor to view the whole class as well.

Teaching methods

Perhaps one of the major pitfalls in teaching a tumbling program is to let one pupil work and the remainder of the class stand in line and observe. Too many instructors line up the entire class at one end of the gymnasium and have them perform individually. This type of class organization leads to discontent and will kill the fun element, with consequent discipline problems. Beginning tumbling lends itself well to the mass method of teaching. Have the class line up along the length of the mats and work across the mats on the command of the instructor. After the class executes one stunt, have them do an about-face and return in the opposite direction while performing the same or another stunt. You will find that the students will not only get more activity out of this type of teaching, but they will also have more fun. It is not uncommon to see the students trying to outdo each other, consequently creating a healthy atmosphere of competition. For most beginning stunts, a maximum of three people can work on a 5' x 10' mat, although two is preferable. More can be accommodated by using shifts of pupils lined up one behind the other.

If the number of mats is insufficient for the whole class, tumbling can also be taught by the squad method. This method combines some other activity or activities with tumbling, and the squads are rotated during the period. Keep in mind that other gymnastic activities probably will require mats also. As the students become more advanced, they will require more space for tumbling and will need more rest between turns. Thus the squad method may be more advantageous for advanced work than the mass method.

Balancing activities can be combine well with tumbling instruction. Both require the same equipment and are organized and conducted in much the same manner. There is some advantage in changing periodically the type of movement; balancing and tumbling provide a good combination for this. After performing two or three rolling movements such as are found in tumbling, it could be restful to execute two or three of the stationary movements found in balancing, and so on. Also, the two activities complement one another. For example, it is helpful to be able to do a forward roll before learning the roll-out ending of a head balance. Similarly, being able to perform a head balance is helpful in learning a headspring.

Evaluation of tumbling probably is best done by use of a stunt chart; this serves to motivate the students as well. For more advanced classes, evaluation could be based on competitive routines.

Safety

Tumbling is a relatively safe activity; however, certain safety procedures should be practised to minimize the risk of injury:

1. Always use mats for tumbling wherever possible. A grassy area or beach could be used for selected stunts.
2. When using more than one mat in a row, one is well advised to secure them together. This will prevent the mats from slipping and leaving "holes" in the tumbling area. Similarly, guard against overlapping of mats, which will cause ridges on which one may turn an ankle.
3. When placing mats, be sure to maintain adequate clearance from walls and obstructions.
4. Inspect the mats to see that there are no ripped places in them where a performer could catch a toe.
5. To make the mats last longer always carry rather than drag them.
6. It is very important that the necessary progression be used in learning tumbling skills. No one learns to run before he or she can walk. By the same token, somersaults cannot be learned before the basic fundamentals can successfully be performed. Too many instructors try to push the ciass too rapidly. This could result in the development of bad habits as well as injury. Fundamentals cannot be stressed too heavily.
7. Students should be encouraged to perform stunts with good form inasmuch as this teaches and indicates control of a stunt as well as adding to the beauty of it.
8. No student should be allowed to perform a new or intricate skill without a spotter until be or she is capable of doing so without danger. Encourage the

students to learn the spotting techniques so that they can help each other.

9. The recent development of thick landing pads adds to the safety of the program; they should be used often.

There are two main methods of spotting: with the hand and with a safety belt. For hand spotting, one spotter gets close to the performer to assist in doing the stunt if necessary and to act in preventing injury if the situation arises. For some stunts two spotters are desirable. A common mistake of spotters is to stay too far away. A person falls quickly, and unless they can step in and catch him or er the spotting is useless. However, the spotter should also be cautioned about standing so close that the performer is hampered. The performer should be watched closely while going through the move so that conditions leading to a fall can be seen as early as possible. Spotters are simply to break a fall and ease the person to the mat, not necessarily holding him or her clear of the mat. The best position for the spotter varies with the stunt. In general, try to figure in which part of the stunt the fall is most likely to occur or where the most help is vital and then station the spotter accordingly. When spotting is particularly important, special directions should be given along with the description of the stunt. For advanced moves spotting is best done with a safety belt. Generally, two people are required to assist by lifting up on the belt. For stunts involving a twist of the body, the ropes must be crossed around the performer in the opposite direction of the way in which the twist is executed unless a twisting belt is used. A travelling overhead belt is very helpful in learning some of the advanced moves.

Program of instruction

The following moves are recommended for learning in the approximate order in which they appear.

1. *Forward roll.* From a squatting position place the hands on the mat about shoulder width apart. Place the chin on the chest and lean forward, pushing with the feet and bending the arms. Allow the back of the shoulders to touch the mat first as the roll is executed and continue rolling on over the back. When the shoulders touch the mat, take the hands from the mat and grasp the shins, pulling the body into a tight tuck. Roll forward in this small ball up to the feet and then straighten to a standing position. The forward roll can also be done with the knees on the outside of the arms. For some pupils, this technique facilitates learning, but the correct and final roll should be done with the knees between the arms.

After learning the technique of doing a roll from a squat, try it from a standing position. More of a forward lean will be evident when going to the mat from a stand. Be sure that the weight of the body is caught by the hands and arms rather than the head or back of the shoulders.

2. *Backward roll.* Start from a squatting position with the hands on the mat and the knees between the arms. Lean forward slightly and then backward into the roll. Push with the hands, sit down, and start to roll onto the back. Place the hands above the shoulders with the fingers pointed back and the palms up. Keep the chin on the chest throughout the roll. Roll over the top of the head and onto the hands, keeping the knees tucked into the chest.

Push with the hands and continue the roll to the feet. Finish in a squat position.

A preliminary move for this stunt is the rocker, which consists of rocking back and forth on the back with the knees in a tuck position and the chin on the chest. Keep the hands over the shoulders, with thumbs toward the heads, and rock partially on them during the rocker. Repeat this rocking motion until you have the feeling of rolling smoothly across the back, and then on one backward roll simply continue on over to the feet. This constitutes a modified backward roll. After learning the technique of doing a roll from a squat position try it from a standing position.

3. *Side roll.* Start from a hands-and-knees position and then place the forearms flat on the mats, assuming a "doggie" position. Roll sideward across the back, holding the knees in toward the chest and continue on over to the hands, forearms, and knees position.
4. *Shoulder roll.* Stand at the edge of the mat with the feet spread slightly. Lean forward and throw the left arm toward the mat, looking between the legs as the arm is thrown. Strike the mat at the elbow first and roll up the arm, across the shoulders and back, and end up on the feet facing sideward. The performer can use the right arm to push up to the feet. After doing this several times, the stunt may be done from a run, simulating the fall that occurs in some games, but in a relaxed and non-injurious way.
5. *Roly poly.* Start by sitting in a straddle position with the legs flat on the mats. Grasp the ankles with each hand. Keeping the arms and legs straight, roll sideward across the back to a sitting position again.

6. *Back extension,* This is a variation of the backward roll, in which the performer momentarily passes through a handstand position and snaps the legs down to the floor. As you push with the hands, you fully extend the arms and shoot the feet upward to a momentary handstand. When in the bandstand position, bend the knees slightly and snap the legs down from the waist. As the legs are snapped down, push with the hands so that the whole body will be completely off the mat. Finish in a standing position.

To practice the snap-down, kick up to a momentary handstand and repeat the last part of the back extension.

7. *Cartwheel.* The cartwheel may be performed either to the left or to the right. It is here described to the left, but may be done to the right by reversing the instructions.

Start with the left side facing down the mat with the legs and arms outstretched and apart like the spokes of a wheel. Rock to the right side by placing the body weight on the right leg and lift the left foot off the ground. Then rock back to the left by placing the body weight on the left leg. With the momentum established by this rocking motion, bend to the left side at the waist and place the left hand on the mat about 2 feet to the side of the left foot. Force the right leg overhead and simultaneously push off the mat with the left leg. As the feet approach the handstand, place the right hand on the mat about shoulder width from the left hand. It is important here that the arms be kept straight and the head tilted back so that the eyes are trained on a spot about 12 inches in front of, and between, the hands. At this point, the body is in a bandstand with the legs held straight and apart and the back arched slightly. As the body passes through the handstand from the side, bring the right foot down on the line established by the left foot and hand by bending to the right at the waist. The left foot will follow to the mat, and one finishes facing the same direction as at the start.

In the event of difficulty in learning the cartwheel, several corrective measures can be taken. First, practice kicking up to a partial bandstand, landing on the opposite foot from the one that was last to leave the mat. This simulates the proper hands-and-feet coordination. The bandstand may be increased in height, and a turn could also be added as proficiency is increased. Next, mark spots on the mat with chalk to show correct placement of each hand and foot, then try the cartwheel in the other direction; many times this will correct the difficulty. If this does not work, start the cartwheel from a squatting tuck position. From there place the left hand on the mat about 1 foot from the left foot. Simply jump and execute a cartwheel, keeping the hands on the mat as described above. Land facing the same direction as at start. Progress by carrying the feet higher overhead until the stunt is done with the body held straight.

If you encounter trouble landing, practice the back end of the cartwheel separately. Kick up to a handstand and bring the right foot down close to the right hand. After the right foot strikes the ground, execute a quarter turn counterclockwise and land with the feet about shoulder width apart. When this can be accomplished successfully, try the cartwheel from the beginning.

8. *One-Arm cartwheel.* In executing the One-Arm cartwheel lean in the direction of the stunt and place the inside hand down and do a cartwheel without using the other arm. At first the stunt may have to be done on a small are basis just as in learning the two-arm cartwheel. As skill progresses it may be done correctly with the legs extended straight overhead and the body straight.

9. *Cartwheel with a quarter turn.* Execute a regular cartwheel and, as the first foot strikes the mat, turn the body a quarter twists bringing the other foot to the mat with the toes pointing in the direction of the momentum. This stunt is an excellent lead-up for a front handspring.

10. *Roundoff.* The roundoff is considered an important key to tumbling because it is used to start the majority of the backward tumbling exercises. The purpose of the roundoff is to change the forward motion of running into backward motion so that backward tumbling stunts may be performed. This stunt may be executed either to the left or to the right, but in this chapter it will be explained to the left.

Take a good run, skip on the right foot, and bring the left foot forward. Place the left foot on the ground, bend forward at the waist, and place the left hand on the mat about 2 feet in front of the left foot. Kick the right foot overhead followed by the left and place the right hand on the mat in front and slightly to the left of the left band. As the stunt progresses the hands and arms pivot in the same direction and the body turns. The fingers of both hands are pointing toward the edge of the mat, When the feet pass overhead, execute a half turn. Snap the feet down from the waist and simultaneously push off the mat by extending the shoulders and flexing the wrists. Land on both feet, facing in the direction opposite from the starting direction. When the feet strike the ground, bound off the balls of the feet. It is important that the eyes be trained on a spot about 6 inches in front of the hands during the entire trick. Placing on chest will mean loss of relative position and inability to complete the roundoff.

The roundoff should be learned from the cartwheel. The two skills are essentially the same, with the exception of the landing. Perform the cartwheel, and instead of facing sideways on the landing, execute a quarter turn more and land on both feet simultaneously.

11. *Neckspring*. From a straight sitting position roll backward, bringing the legs overhead to a pike position, and place the hands on the mats behind the shoulders with the fingers pointing toward the shoulders and the thumbs by the ears. From this position on the shoulders roll forward and at the same time: (a) whip the legs forward at about a 60° angle and arch the back; and (b) push off the mat with the hands and back of the bead, Continue the whip of the legs until the body lands in a squat position on the feet.

Before trying the kip in its entirety, first try a bridge position on the shoulders and feet. This Will give the feeling of lifting the hips. Then go to the bridge from the kip position on the back of the shoulders using the kipping action. When this can be accomplished successfully, try the neekspring as described above. A technique using a partner to learn this stunt is as follows: Have one person sit on the mats with the knees flexed ' the hands behind the hips, and the feet flat on the mats. The person trying the neckspring lies on the mat the with his head between the spotter's legs and his shoulders resting on the lifting partner's feet, grasping the partner at the inside of the ankles with the thumbs. The performer rolls backward, lifting his hips with his legs coming near the partner's head, From this position lie should then execute the neckspring technique of whipping the legs upward and forward while the assisting partner lifts his legs, thus pushing the performer's shoulders upward, which helps the completion of the neckspring.

12. *Headspring.* Take a slight run, hurdle, and land on mat with both feet at the same time. Place both hands on the mat with the top of the head about 6 inches in front of the hands as though doing a headstand. Push off the feet, keeping the body in a deep piked position with the legs straight. The hips are carried over the head until the body weight falls off balance down the mat. Whip the legs overhead from the waist and on toward the mat in one continuous arc, simultaneously pushing with the hands. Land on the feet with the knees bent slightly, depending on how high the headspring is executed. This skill is not done by kicking or pushing the feet from the knees but rather by snapping or whipping the legs out of the piked position from the waist.

The headspring should first be learned from a rolled mat and with the use of a spotter. First try the headspring from a standing position. Place the hands on the near side on top of the rolled mat, with the head on the far side as though going to a headstand. Move the feet close to the mat roll, keeping the body in a deep pike position until the body weight is off balance down the mat. At this point whip the feet overhead from the waist and then down to the mat in one continuous arch, simultaneously pushing with the hands. Land on the feet. Once mastered from a mat roll, the stunt can he performed on a level mat as described above. The same bridging technique used in learning the neckspring is suggested in learning the headspring.

The spotter sits on the mat roll. As the performer places his or her hands on the rolled-up mat, the spotter grasps the performer's upper arm with one hand, places the other hand under the upper back, and assists him or her through the stunt.

13. *Front handspring.* Take a good run, skip on the right foot, and bring the left foot forward. Place left foot on the mat, bend forward at the waist, and place both hands about 2 feet ahead of the left foot. Kick the right foot overhead, followed by the left. As the feet are being carried overhead, the arms should be held straight and the eyes trained on a spot about 6 inches in front of the hands. As the body passes through the handstand position, push off the mat with the shoulders and wrists without bending the arms. Continue on over to the feet and land with the knees flexed.

Like the headspring, the handspring should be learned with a mat roll and with the use of spotters. Start from a standing position. Place the hands on the mat in front of the rolled mat, and with the aid of spotters kick up to a handstand. Arch over the rolled mat. Two spotters should assist the performer throughout this arch. Do this arch over the mat several times to establish the feeling of turning over, with the arms straight, back arched, and so on. Then try the stunt with a small run and execute a front handspring over the rolled mat. The position of the spotter is to sit straddling the rolled mat or kneeling in front of it. As the performer places his hands on the mat, grasp the upper arm with one hand and place the other hand behind his shoulders. As he overbalances, assist him to a landing position on the feet.

Another method of learning the handspring is to walk up to a landing pad that is about 12 inches thick and place the head and bands on the pad. Then kick up into a headstand position but carry the legs over into an arched wrestler's bridge position. The coach should emphasize that the performer should not touch any part of the back or shoulders until after the feet have landed. At that time the body may relax and drop to the back. Do several of these and then try it with a small run and a little stronger kick of the lead leg and push of the bands so that the body springs lightly up and over onto the feet prior to falling back onto the back side of the body. After many of these attempts with continued strong emphasis on the arch, the performer should finish on his or her feet in a standing position. The final skill is done without the head touching and with a good run, a strong whip of the leg, and a forceful push of the hands.

Some students may learn the front handspring more easily by using the following :technique with a partner:

Have one person stand on the mat facing the performer. The performer kicks into a handstand with the partner catching his legs at the calves. This is repeated several times with a stronger kick each time, with the partner catching the legs surely with each kick. After this his been done several times, the partner then grasps the performer by the hips and allows the performer's back to ride slightly over his shoulders. With confidence the partner will eventually lift the performer slightly from the mats but ~always place him back to his bands in the direction from which he came. This develops the feeling of kicking the legs upward with the arms straight and the back slightly arched, essential parts of a good front handspring. After the above Has been done several times, the performer attempts the handspring with the spotter stepping to one side and simply lifting him over as he executes the stunt.

14. *Tinsica.* Start by taking a good run, skip on the right foot, and bring the left foot forward. Place the left foot on the mat and by bending forward from the waist, place the left hand about 2 feet in front of the left foot, simultaneously kicking the right leg overhead followed by the left and place the right hand on the mat about 6 inches in front of, and about shoulder width from, the left hand. The arms should be held straight, and the eyes should be trained on a spot about 18 inches ahead of the hands. The legs pass overhead and the right foot lands about two feet ahead of the right hand, with the left foot following and landing about 18 inches ahead of the right foot. When this trick is completed the performer should be facing in the same direction as the starting position.

The tinsica may easily be learned by using the cartwheel as a lead-up stunt. At the completion of the cartwheel as the left foot nears the mat, execute a quarter turn and come to a standing position facing down the mats. Repeat this until the quarter twist comes easily.

15. *Forward somersault.* Take a good run, skip on the left foot, bring the right foot forward, simultaneously raise both arms overhead, and land on the mat with both feet at the same time (hurdle). It is important here that the hurdle be short and fast so that the forward motion established by running may be directed upward. Throw the arms upward, forward, and downward and place the chin on the chest while lifting the hips. Continue the circular motion with the hands by grasping and pulling the shins into a tuck position. The chest should be close to the knees and the heels close to the buttocks. After completing the somersault, shoot out of the tuck and land in a standing position on the mat.

The forward somersault can easily be learned by stacking mats on top of each other to a height of about three feet. Take a good run, hurdle, and lift into a forward roll onto the stack of mats. Continue this action until the roll becomes easy. Progress by taking the weight off the hands until the roll can be completed without touching the hands to the mat. From here try the front somersault to, a sitting position on the stack of mats. When this is completed successfully, take the mats away one at a time and try to finish standing on the feet after completing the somersault. Another method of teaching a front somersault is to provide a rolled-up mat over which the performer executes a front somersault with the spotter sitting on the mat assisting throughout the stunt. The trampoline can also be used effectively to teach the fundamentals of a good forward somersault. '

Still another method of learning a front somersault is with the use of a tumbling belt and two spotters. The spotters simply run alongside the performer and help him through the stunt by lifting up on the belt as the somersault is executed A springboard trampoline can also assist the performer if spotted by this method.

When spotting this stunt without the use of a safety belt, the spotter stands at the takeoff point, placing one hand beneath the performer's head or shoulders to insure a good tuck and to lift him if needed. The other hand should grab the upper arm to prevent an overspin.

Variation: Forward Somersault—Russian Technique. Prior to taking off from the mats, swing, the straight arms downward and backward past the hips, keeping the body erect with the chest up. After the arms have swung past the hips, duck the head toward the chest and begin the somersault. Grasp the underside of the thighs, pulling the knees tightly into the body. Continue the somersault to the feet.

16. *Tigna. A* tigna is a type of front somersault following a tinsica in that the takeoff is from one foot. The body somersaults in a semituck position.

17. *Back handspring. This is* one of the more advanced tumbling stunts and should not be attempted without a spotter.

Start from a standing position with the feet about shoulder width apart and with the arms held straight out in front of the body. Swing the arms downward, simultaneously bend the knees, and sit back as though sitting in a chair. As the body falls off balance backward, swing the arms upward overhead, simultaneously forcing the head backward. Straighten the legs and push off the mat with the toes. As you push off with the feet, force the hips upward and make a big circle with the hands. As the hands land on the mat with the fingers turned in slightly and the arms bent a little, the body is approaching a handstand position. From this position with a little hollow of the chest, snap the legs down from the waist, pushing with the arms, and land in a standing position. It is important that you continue to force the arms over in the arc until they finally reach the mat.

When spotting by the hand method, the two spotters should take a position on the knees or simply standing on the mat at the side of the performer. Have the performer do a back bend and assist by supporting his body weight. When he is in the back bend position, have him keep his arms straight and force his head back so that he is looking at a spot about 12 inches in front of his hands. Carry his feet overhead so that he passes through the handstand position. Have the performer then come to a stand on the mat by bending down from the waist. Repeat this several times until he gets the idea of turning over. Progress by having him try the back handspring in its entirety.

To hand spot the back handspring in its entirety, place the right hand in the small of the performer's back and use the left hand to assist him in turning over. This may be accomplished by lifting him behind the thighs with the left hand as he starts the back handspring and flipping his feet overhead. When using this method of spotting, it is important to stand close to the performer because it may be impossible to support his body weight at arm's length.

A tumbling safety belt may also be used for spotting purposes in first learning this stunt. Two spotters may then assist the performer through the back-bend action as mentioned previously.

After learning the handspring from a standing position, try it from a snap-down. This involves kicking into a momentary bandstand and snapping the feet down vigorously while pushing off from the fingers. This brings the performer back into a standing position with the momentum already started for a back handspring.

A good technique for teaching a back handspring that follows in line with a roundoff back handspring is as follows: Have the performer stand on the mats with knees slightly bent, back straight, and arms overhead. Two spotters, one standing on each side, grasp hands behind the performer's back, with the free hands prepared to lift the legs. The performer then slowly leans backward, placing his hands on the mat, and the spotters hold the performer off the mat and at the same time lift the performer's legs through the back handspring movement. The performer, after passing through the handstand, snaps the feet downward to the mat to finish in a standing position. In succeeding attempts, the performer should obtain more spring from the legs and throw his head and arms backward more vigorously, which in turn will make the completion of the back handspring easier. After successfully completing one back handspring, the performer should try two or more in sequence.

18. *Back somersault.* The standing back somersault should not be attempted without a spotter. Start from a standing position with the feet about shoulder width apart and the arms banging in a natural position at the sides. Bend the knees, swing the arms downward, and jump up, swinging the arms overhead as though catching a horizontal bar. Throw the bead and arms backward hard, simultaneously bringing the knees up to the chest. Circle the arms sideways to grasp the shins, pulling the body into a tight tuck. It is important to pull the knees to the chest bard, continually forcing the head backward. Land on the feet in a standing position.

Before trying the back somersault in its entirety, first attempt the jump tuck. From a standing position, jump into the air and bring the knees up to the chest. As the knees strike the chest grasp the shins and bold the tuck position. It is important here to bring the knees up to the chest rather than the chest down to the knees. Shoot out of the tuck and land on the feet. Do not throw the head and arms backward when practising this lead-up stunt as it can cause partial turnover and possible injury. A spotter may assist here by standing behind the performer and simply placing a hand on his back to prevent overspring. After this jump tuck has been tried several times, try the back somersault with the use of a spotter or two.

In spotting this stunt, it is suggested that two spotters be utilized, one on each side of the performer. As the performer tries the back somersault the spotters should assist by supporting the performer in the small of the back, holding him up. At the same time throw his legs over into the back somersault with the other hand. Spot very carefully during the early stages of this skill.

19. *Roundoff—Back Handspring.* Take a good run and execute the roundoff as described earlier. It is important here to push of the hands on the roundoff so that the entire body is in the air at one point. As the feet are snapped downward, they should be pulled well under the body to impart back motion. Before the feet land on the roundoff, the back handspring should be started. The hands should come off the floor during the roundoff and be carried as though making a big circle. Keep the arms straight and continue the circle so that the hands will be forward of the center of gravity of the body when they reach the mat. Snap the legs down from the waist, as in doing a snap-down, and come to a stand on the mat.

Do not attempt this trick without a spotter. The method used in spotting may again be determined by the size of the performer. A small boy or girl may successfully be hand spotted. Larger individuals should be spotted with the use of a safety belt and two spotters. It is important that the spotters be experienced; otherwise injury may result.

20. *Roundoff—Back somersault.* Take a good run and execute a roundoff as described earlier. It is important that the feet *are not* pulled through on the roundoff but are instead kicked out backward so that the backward motion established by the roundoff can be directed upward. The arms should move off the mat directly from the roundoff and be carried upward and overhead. As the feet leave the

mat, bring the knees up to the chest (tuck) and simultaneously throw the head backward. As the knees are forced up to the chest, the arms complete a small circle and grasp the shins. When one revolution is complete, shoot out of the tuck and land. The back somersault should be taken high and spun fast to give more time for the landing. In order to increase the rate of spin, think about kicking the chin with the knees as the tuck is made. While in the tuck, pull the knees up tight to the chest and force the toes overhead.

The roundoff—back somersault should not be attempted without spotters. It is suggested here that the safety belt and two spotters be used for this stunt.

21. *Roundoff—Back handspring—Back somersault.* Take a good run and execute a roundoff and back handspring as previously described. Snap off the hands on the roundoff and pull the feet under the body for the back handspring. The landing on the handspring is very important because it will determine the height of the back somersault. With a long, low back handspring the legs are extended back so as to effect a blocking action, and the arms are lifted upward very swiftly into the back somersault. If the handspring is high and no block is made with the legs, the back somersault becomes low and long. As the feet leave the floor, bring the knees up to the chest into a tight 'tuck and simultaneously throw the head backward. Complete one somersault and shoot out of the tuck for the landing.

The roundoff—back handspring—back somersault should not be attempted without a spotter. The hand belt, with two spotters running alongside the performer, should be used when this skill is attempted.

Twisting tumbling

For the purpose of continuity, all twisting moves will be explained from the roundoff and handspring, and to the right. These moves should not be attempted until the roundoff—handspring back somersault can be completed successfully and should be attempted only with a spotter. The twisting belt should be used in learning all twisting moves.

1. *Half twisting backward somersault.* Start by taking a good run and execute a roundoff—back handspring. It is important here that you kick out on the back handspring so that the half twister is carried high. As the feet land on the back handspring, carry the arms overhead and force the hips high as though doing a layout back somersault—with the body completely straight. Carry the head backward and then to the right side, simultaneously dropping the right shoulder and arm and bringing the left arm across the chest. Complete the back somersault with one half twist and land on the feet. It is important that the head and shoulders are forced over the body on landing, Failure to do this will result in underturning the somersault, causing a sit-down landing.

2. *Full twisting backward somersault.* As the feet land on the back hand-spring carry the left arm upward and over the right shoulder, simultaneously carrying the right shoulder and elbow backward and downward. The head moves backward and to the right, looking over the right shoulder. For best results the mat should be seen over the right

shoulder as the twist starts and remain visible throughout the twist. The body is in a layout position with the head remaining in one spot and acting as an axis around which the body rotates. After the initial throw, bring the arms into the chest to increase the rate of spin. On completing one revolution, force the arms away from the chest to stop the spin and land on the feet.

Another technique used on back twisting is to lift upward swiftly with the arms but place the body in a hollow-chest layout position with the head slightly forward and chin down. This will tend to place the body in a straight line and increase the efficiency of twisting. Lift the body straight up and in twisting to the right after both arms reach upward, the right arm is dropped toward the right shoulder and the left arm drives across the body, activating the twist. The head remains downward and looks in the direction of the right armpit. Keep the body straight and taut.

Routines

Innumerable combinations are possible and there is much value in allowing the performers to put together their own combinations into a longer routine. Some suggestions follow:

1. Alternating diving rolls with low tight rolls.
2. Forward roll—cross legs into backward roll.
3. Alternate two-arm cartwheel with one-arm cartwheel.
4. Series of cartwheels.
5. Cartwheel into a roundoff into a back extension.

6. Handspring to headspring into a forward roll.
7. Series of headsprings.
8. Series of cartwheels with a one-quarter turn.
9. Series of tinsicas.
10. Front somersault—forward roll—headspring.
11. Roundoff—two or three back hand-springs.
12. Tinsica—roundoff—back handspring—back flip.
13. Roundoff—back handspring—back somersault—back handspring—back somersault.
14. Roundoff into successive back somersaults.

Double tumbling

Doubles tumbling consists simply of two persons executing tumbling feats together. This activity can be a great deal of fun and extremely rewarding. It does require close cooperation between the two performers, however, and it is also suggested that at least one and possibly two spotters should assist the performers. Some of the doubles tumbling stunts include:

1. *Doubles forward roll.* Start with one partner lying on the mat with his feet in the air while the other stands at his head in a straddle position. The partners grasp each other's ankles. Then the top person dives forward into a forward roll taking the bottom person's feet down toward the mat with him. The roll brings the bottom performer up onto his feet and he in turn dives forward. 'Men the other is on top again and they continue in a steady roll down the mat.

2. *Doubles backward roll.* Start in, the same position as the doubles forward roll. The top person sits down, pulling' the bottom person's feet back with him' The bottom performer executes a backward roll, pushing up vigorously with his hands. Thus, the positions of both~ performers are now reversed, and the, stunt may be continued in a steady roll backward down the mat.
3. *Log rolls.* Start with three persons kneeling, on the mat parallel with one another. The middle performer rolls sideways to the left and at the same time the left outside person jumps sideways over the rolling body to the center position landing he immediately rolls sideways to the right, and at the same the outside right man jumps sideways over the rolling body into the center and then proceeds to roll sideways to the left. At this time the outside left person will jump sideways to the right then roll. This log roll action can be for as long as desired.
4. *Triple rolls.* Start three persons standing on the mat with the outer persons facing the middle and the middle one facing the left outside person. The middle person performs a tight forward roll toward the outside person, who in turn straddle-leaps over the rolling body to the center position; on landing on his feet he immediately squats into a tight forward roll in the direction of the right outside performer. At this moment the right outside performer straddle-leaps over the rolling body, landing on his feet in the center position, and then proceeds to do a forward roll to the outside, whereupon the outside man straddle-leaps over the

rolling body into the center position. This action can be repeated for as long as desired.

5. *Knee and Shoulder* Spring. The bottom person lies on his back with his knees raised and slightly spread. The top person approaches toward the other's feet and with a short run places his hands on the bottom person's knees. As the top person performs a headspring motion the bottom one assists him by placing his bands on the shoulder blades of the top performer. The top person continues over and lands on his feet just beyond the head of the bottom person.

6. *Back to Back Toss. In* this stunt one person tosses the other person over his back. Start standing back to back with the hands clasped over the shoulders. One person bends his knees, then leans forward and proceeds to lift the other person over his back. The thrower, or bottom person, should be sure to dip slightly with his knees so that the top person's buttocks rest against the lower back of the bottom man. The thrower should stop his forward lean and raise up as be feels the top person rolling off his back. The top person should continue to pike the body until ready to land. Be sure to have a spotter available throughout the early learning phases of this stunt.

7. *Front flip pitch.* Start with both performers standing, facing the same direction. The flyer bends one knee and small dip in their knees and then the flyer proceeds to lift for a forward somersault, with the thrower lifting hard on the top person's shin and instep, flyer, with the aid of the lift, should then execute a forward somersault.

8. *Side leg back flip pitch.* The flyer places his straight leg into the thrower's hand and places his right hand on the thrower's shoulders. The thrower lifts the leg up into the air and with the aid of the other hand on the flyer's back throws him into a back flip. The flyer should keep the lifted leg taut so that the thrower will have a solid means of lifting him into the air.
9. *Back flip toe pitch.* This is done by the flyer placing his hands on the thrower's shoulders and setting one foot in the thrower's hands. The flyer then straightens upwards and backward into back somersault pitch. The thrower lifts upward into the air and throws the flyer into somersault. Be sure to use a spotter in learning this stunt.
10. *Doubles cartwheel. This* consists of two persons executing a double cartwheel with one person's legs on the ground while the other's are in the air. One person stands with his legs slightly bent in straddle position with the arms to the side and front of the body. The other performer approaches from the side of the standing person and thrusts his head between the person's legs with the shoulders resting on the top side of the thighs. The bands grab the back side of the standing person Is legs. At the same time the standing person circles the top person's waist in preparing to execute the double cartwheel. The top person should swing the forward foot around to the ground as quickly as possible in order to lift the standing person over into the second cartwheel. The two should hold tightly to each other; this will insure the completion of the double cartwheel. The spotter should stand behind and assist by lifting each performer's waist.

11. *Assisted back flip over arm.* The thrower should place one arm across the waist of the performer and the other hand under the back side of the knees. The performer grasps the top arm of the thrower and prepares for the back flip. The performer kicks both legs and knees upward and around the arm of the thrower, in a manner similar to kicking over a bar in the playground. The thrower lifts and turns the performer around his arm as pictured.

12. *Back flip off partner's feet.* One person is in a supine position with the legs elevated. The other person stands in a straddle position over the bottom person's legs and hips, facing away. The bottom person places his feet in the small of the back of the performer as the performer leans backward into an arch position. The bottom person grasps the performer's shoulders as he leans backward, and when the shoulders are over the bottom person's face and his weight well over the bottom person's feet, the top person then continues over in a flip action to a stand on the other side of the bottom person's head. Do slowly at first, like a slow arch backbend (handspring technique), until the timing is learned, and then more of a flipping action can be incorporated into the stunt. A good push with the bottom person's legs gives height and excitement to the stunt.

13. *Wheelbarrow pitch to forward somersault.* The performer assumes a push-up position with the body elevated from the mat by straight arms and with the legs extended backward into the thrower's hands. With a beat consisting of an extension of the performer's waist and a slight dip in the thrower's

bands, the flyer then whips his hips upward and over and then ducks his head and commences the forward somersault. The thrower lifts vigorously with his arms (hands under the performer's feet) and thus assists the performer in the forward somersault to his feet. The performer must be sure to wait before beginning the forward somersault turn until the thrower has had an opportunity to lift forcefully upward; with this waiting time, success is sure to occur. Another version of this stunt is done with the performer in a handstand position; be then falls down into the thrower's hands and does the forward somersault.

14. *Ankle pick-Up.* The performer lies on his back and extends the legs straight up, placing the hands on the mat behind the shoulders. The thrower steps in close to the performer's hips and grasps the uplifted ankles with the thumbs on the inside of the ankles. The performer bends his knees slightly and then extends them upward at the same time the thrower lifts forcefully upward and then activates a throw of the feet over and beyond the flyer's head. The performer continues this back extension action on over to his feet. With proper timing, a good lift by the thrower, and a good push by the performer, the ankle pick-up can be executed at a fascinating height, particularly if the thrower is taller than the performer. This stunt can be done from a handstand position, with the thrower standing behind the performer grasping the uplifted ankles. From here the performer simply ducks his head and lowers his shoulders downward into a partial forward roll. When the performer reaches his back, he bends his knees slightly and then proceeds back

upward into the back extension action with the thrower lifting him upward and over to his feet.

15. *Sitting assisted back flip.* The thrower sits on the mat with his legs in straddle position and his hands flat on the mat, palms upward, while the performer stands on the thrower's hands. As the thrower lifts upward with his hands, the *performer executes* a backward somersault. The thrower gives an assist to the performer in the completion of the backward flip. A spotter should stand at the side to assist the performer.
16. *Assisted front somersault.* The performer stands between two spotters, the and all face the same direction. The inside hands of the spotters grasp the wrists of the performer, and the outside of hands grip the performer's upper arms. Then after a few steps the performer jumps into a forward somersault, and the spotters, lifting on their respective arms, assist the performer in the completion of the flip. Be sure the spotters do not lift too fast or too high, because this prevents the performer from turning into the somersault action, Also, the spotters should continue to lift the performer even after the somersault has been *completed, This* will allow for a soft landing on the feet instead of slamming into the mats.

7

BALANCING

We all have seen children in the playground, front lawn, or sandy beach kick upward into a momentary handstand, and each second that the balance is held is a moment of joy for them. It is great fun and a matter of warm pride to accomplish a balance of some sort with a moderate degree of proficiency. Besides this aspect of fun, balancing does contribute a great deal to the physical development of the growing boy or girl. Very little equipment or space is required; the regular tumbling mat is satisfactory for all degrees of balancing stunts. Surely an activity that offers so much return on so little investment of equipment and space should be given serious consideration in the physical education program. Balancing as such does not lend itself to organized competition, although it plays a large part in other gymnastic competitive events, such as floor exercise and parallel bars.

Values

The specific values of balancing activities are:

1. Balancing develops coordination and agility. The ability to manoeuvre the body in an upside-down position and to land correctly on the feet requires a great deal of coordinated action from the entire body.

2. Strength and endurance are developed by many balancing stunts. Many balances call for holding the body in positions that depend on muscular action for support, particularly of the abdomen and shoulders. Presses often depend on strength in the arms and shoulders.
3. Balance and a sense of relocation are essential in balancing stunts and are gained through consistent practice. Poise and orientation can be developed through balancing activities.
4. Balancing develops confidence and sureness in the ability to handle the body. This is a value that all growing boys and girls should experience.
5. In executing the doubles balancing stunts, a certain degree of teamwork is necessary. This value is developed as one performer depends on another to do his or her part of the stunt.
6. Balancing is fun and enjoyable because it is a natural and self-motivating activity.
7. Balancing provides a chance for the small boy or girl to gain needed recognition, Very often the smaller person has an advantage in balancing over the larger person, making balancing different from many sports.

Organization

Balancing needs little equipment. Tumbling mats and space are about the only essential requirements, and even if tumbling mats are not available the activity can still be conducted if handled with close supervision and caution. Any area can be used, including a gymnasium, classroom, school corridors, and playgrounds. The important item in this respect is to provide ample space for each student. There is little difference in the organization and conduct of tumbling and balancing. Only the differences will be noted here, and the reader is asked to refer to the preceding chapter on tumbling for the general plan.

Balancing can be taught by the mass method or by the squad method. Unlike tumbling, it requires no more space for advanced stunts than for beginning stunts. Balancing work requires a lot of practice for most people, so enough time should be allotted for it. However, variety is also needed to maintain interest. Tumbling and a mixture of singles and doubles balancing can make a good contribution to variety. It is not necessary for singles balancing to precede doubles balancing. Both can be presented in the same lesson.

For singles balancing, the students should work in pairs, with one performing and the other spotting. For doubles balancing, groups of three or four are best, with two students performing the stunt and the other students spotting.

Students should be encouraged to perform stunts with good form inasmuch as this teaches, and indicates control of, the stunt as well as adding to the beauty of it.

Program of instruction

The following stunts are recommended for learning in the approximate order in which they appear. The singles work will be presented first followed by the i doubles balancing stunts.

Singles balancing

1. *Squat head balance.* Start this stunt from a squat position with the hands on the mat and the inside of the knees resting on the elbows. From this position lean forward and place the head on the mat. Lift the toes from the mat so that the balance is on the head and hands, thus placing the performer in the squat head balance.

Variation: Do a squat head balance; lift the knees off the elbows, touch them together, and then place them back on the elbows.

2. *Squat hand balance.* This is similar to the squat bead balance except the head does not touch the mat and the entire balance is maintained by the hands. Start from a squat position with the arms at shoulder-width apart and the inside of the knees resting on the elbows. Lean forward, keeping the head off the :mat, and lift the feet into the balance position. Maintain the balance by working with the arms and pressing with the fingers.

Variation: While doing a squat hand balance, lift the knees off the elbows, touch them together, and then place them back on the elbows. (For a challenge, see if the students can do this several times without losing their balance.)

3. *Head balance.* This stunt consists of balancing on the head and hands with the feet straight overhead. One method of moving into the head balance is from the squat head balance position. After reaching the balancing point on this fundamental stunt, raise the feet upward over the head. Do this slowly and the balance will be maintained more

easily. Another method is to place the head and hands in the proper position on the mat and simply kick one leg up, and follow with the other into the head balance position. Be sure to maintain a triangular formation with the head and the hands and keep the back neatly arched. Also, rest the head on the forward part and not the very top or back side of the head.

It is suggested that a spotter be used while learning this stunt. The best position for the spotter is to the side and slightly behind the performer. To come down from this stunt, either duck the head and do a forward roll or return the legs to the mat in the same manner as they were put in position.

Variation: While doing a head balance, lift the hands from the mat and clap them together and then place them back on the mats and maintain the head balance.

4. *Forward roll to head balance.* Do a forward roll, and on reaching the feet remain in a tuck position and place the hands on the mat well ahead of the feet, lean forward, and reach outward with the bead before placing it on the mat. Then slowly move the feet up into the balance position. Rushing into the balance out of the roll will simply cause the performer to fall forward into another you.

5. *Head balance arms folded.* Start from a kneeling position with the arms folded in front or the chest and resting on the mats. Place the head beyond the arms and kick upward into the balance position.

6. *Head and forearm balance.* From a kneeling position place the forearms flat on the mat, with the thumbs of the bands almost touching each other. Place the

head in the cup formed by the thumb and fingers of the two hands and kick upward into the bead and forearm balance. This same stunt may also be done with the fingers interlaced behind the head. In either method be sure that the forearms and head form a good tripod.

7. *Forearm balance.* From a head and forearm balance, lift the head off the mat and maintain the balance with the forearms alone. The Position may also be attained by placing the forearms on the mat and kicking upward into the balance position without the head touching the mat at all. Keep the upper arms as vertical as possible and the lower arms nearly parallel to each other.

8. *Backward Roll to Head Balance.* From a sitting position on the mat, roll backward as in a backward roll. When the back of the head touches the mat i place the hands beside the head and extend the legs upward, Continue the roll to the top of the head, arch the back, and at the same time slide the hands backward to the tripod position to stop the momentum of the moving body and to secure the head balance.

9. *Hand balance.* This stunt consists of simply balancing oneself in an inverted position on the hands. It is a fascinating stunt but requires a great deal of practice before final accomplishment.

There are several methods of learning this stunt. One of the most basic is to do it next to a flat surface such as a wall. It is advisable to use a spotter while first learning this stunt, even though support will be received from the wall. Place a mat near the wall and put the hands on the mat, shoulder-width apart, with the fingers pointing forward a short distance from the wall. With head up and eves focused on the wall, kick upward until the feet rest on the wall. While kicking into the hand balance be sure to keep the head up to prevent the body from rolling into the wall. From this resting position push gently away from the wall with one foot in order to move slowly into a freely supported hand balance. The action is a back-and-forth motion from a free hand balance to the wall band balance.

Another method consists of working in an open area with the use of a spotter. Execute the stunt in the same manner and let the spotter grab the legs and hold the performer in a hand balance position. Little by little the spotter can release the legs of the performer and finally a freely supported hand balance will be accomplished. It is most important that the spotter work in extremely close to the performer and safely hold him in position. A safe recovery may be made from an overbalance by turning the body a quarter turn and landing on the feet. In the final hand balance, keep the head between the arms (eyes looking at the hands '.. back stretched, and bands pointed forward, with fingers gripping the floor and arms straight.

10. *Walk on hands.* Walking on the hands is sometimes easier than holding a fixed hand balance, although a controlled walk is really more difficult. After getting into a hand balance, simply lean forward, and before overbalancing too far, move one hand at a time forward a short distance. A constant lean will provide a smooth walk. Avoid taking too large a step with the bands.

11. *Double elbow lever.* Start from a kneeling position With the hands on the floor so that the fingers point toward the knees. Lean forward and place the right hip on the right elbow and then the left hip on the left elbow. From this position extend the legs backward until they are straight, then raise them slightly from the mat. The body then will be supporting itself in a double elbow lever position.

12. *Single elbow lever.* Start from a kneeling position with the right hand on the floor, fingers pointing toward the knees, and the right elbow inside the right hip. The left hand is on the floor, extended beyond the head. Extend the legs backward, either together or in a straddle position, and raise the feet from the floor, thus placing most of the weight on the right elbow. Gradually shift the entire weight to the right elbow and slowly lift the left hand from the floor. The body will then be supporting itself in a single elbow lever position.

13. *One-arm hand balance.* To learn this difficult stunt, start from an ordinary hand balance. Slowly shift weight from two arms to one arm and at the same time lift the other hand from the floor. Keep the balancing arm straight and strong, with the other hand ready to add support from the floor if necessary to maintain balance. The legs may be kept together or in a straddle position. Practice is the key to the final learning of the one-arm handstand.

Doubles balancing

Doubles balancing is a very enjoyable activity and can readily supplement a singles balancing program. Many of the stunts are relatively easy, and with a third or fourth person to assist and spot, the activity can become fun and exciting. Some of the stunts could include:

1. *Chest balance.* Start this stunt with one partner kneeling, on all fours. The other partner slides his arms under the kneeling partners chest and places his chest on the kneeling partner's back. Then the top person kicks upward as if kicking into a head balance, and finishes in a chest balance position on the partner's back. The arms could also be placed so one is along the kneeling partner's leg and the other along the partner's arm.

2. *Hold out, facing out.* Start this stunt by having both persons face the same direction. Then the bottom person squats down, bends forward, and places his head between the top person's legs and lifts him into a sitting position on his shoulders. The top person then places the feet on the bottom person's thighs,, with toes pointed downward, and the bottom person places his hands just above the top person's knees. The one on the bottom leans backward and removes his head from between the legs and finishes by holding the top person on his thighs with his arms straight. The top person straightens upward and forces a neat arch in the body with the arms out horizontally, head and chest erect. To dismount from this position, the top person simply drops forward to his feet. The spotter should stand in front of the performers in assisting in this stunt.

One may also mount into the position by jumping

up onto the bottom person's thighs with bottom person lifting by the hips.

3. *Hold out, facing in.* The two partners stand facing each other. The top person circles his hands behind the bottom person's neck while the bottom one places his hands behind the top person's hips. The top person then proceeds to step upward onto thighs of the bottom person with the toes facing outward, keeping the hips over the feet as he steps up. When a solid balance position is reached, each right arm is brought across the other's chest and a sure grip is secured on the other's wrist. From this position, both lean backward slightly and finish up in the hold-out-facing-in position. Some find it easier to grasp right arms as part of the starting position and simply to step up onto the bottom person's thighs and proceed to lean into the hold out, facing in.

4. *Knee and shoulder balance.* One partner is in a supine position with the hands and knees raised and the feet on the mat close to the buttocks. The top person places his hands on the bottom one's knees and his shoulders in the bottom person's hands. From this position, he kicks upward into a knee and shoulder balance. Be sure that the top person's arms are kept straight through out this stunt and that contact is made with the shoulders into the bottom person's hands before kicking upward into the balance. The spotter can stand by the side of the performers to assist in reaching the balance position.

5. *Front swan on feet.* One partner lies in a supine position with the legs and hands raised. The top

person faces his partner and places his pelvis on the bottom person's feet, the latter's heels angling in toward the stomach and the toes, outward. Both grasp each others hands. Then the top person leans forward into an arched balance position on the feet. He holds the hands until the balance is secure and then releases the grip and lifts the arms gracefully to the side supported by the bottom person's feet.

6. *Back swan on feet.* This is similar to the front swan except the top person is balanced on his back. The top partner backs into the upraised feet of the bottom one and leans backward into the back swan on the latter's feet. The bottom person's heels are inward and the toes pointed outward; the feet rest on the hips and the small of the upper person's back.

7. *Foot-to-hand balance.* The bottom person lies on his back with hands beside the head and legs raised upward. The top person stands lightly on the bottom one's hands and grasps the uplifted feet. The top person jumps upward slightly and pushes downward on the bottom one's feet. Simultaneously, the bottom person lifts the hands straight to a straight-arm position. When this foot-to-hand position is secure the top person released the bottom one's feet and gets up into a comfortable standing position

8. *Two-high stand.* The partners stand facing in the same direction. The person's hands rest just above his shoulders and the top person stands behind him, grasping the bottom person's hands as in a handshake. The top one then moves to the side of the bottom person, who squats down a little. From

this position, the top partner places his right foot on the bottom one's thigh and proceeds to climb upward onto the shoulders. The bottom partner pulls with the arms and keeps both arms firm and strong while the top partner is approaching the final position. When the top person's foot is on the far shoulder of the bottom one, the other foot is removed from the bottom one's thigh and placed on the other shoulder. The hands are still clasped, and after a good balance position is obtained the hands are released and the bottom person's hands are placed behind the top one's knees, just above the calf. The top person's shins should be resting on the back side of the bottom one's bead, and the bottom one's hands then in effect pull downward and forward on the top person's legs. This makes for a solid two-high stand, To dismount, the bottom person lifts his right hand, the top person grasps it and proceeds to leap forward, turning slightly to his right as be leaps to the ground. Another method is simply to jump forward off the shoulders to the mat. As skill progresses, the two persons may want to finish the dismount by doing forward rolls after the top person lands on the mat.

Be sure to work with one or more spotters on this stunt. The spotter should be behind the top person while he is climbing up to the shoulders and assist by pushing upward under the buttocks.

9. *Shoulder balance on feet.* The bottom person is in a supine position with the hands and feet raised. The top person stands behind his head, grasps the bottom partner's bands, and places his shoulders in the bottom partners feet. The top person then

jumps upward in a tuck position and continues to press upward into the shoulder balance on the feet. Pressure is applied to the hands in order to complete the press to the balance. When the shoulder balance on the feet is secure, the hands are released and the top person places his hands on the lower legs of the bottom one and continues to hold the shoulder balance on the feet. This same balance can be done in the opposite direction, with the top person starting from a position behind the buttocks.

10. *Low arm-to-arm balance.* The bottom person is in a supine position with the arms up and the legs straight out on the mat, while the top person straddles the bottom man's waist, leans forward, and places his upper arms in the bottom one's hands. The top person grasps the back side of the bottom one's arms; be then jumps upward into a tuck position and continues to press into a low arm-to-arm. This position can also be reached by kicking upward with one leg, followed by the other. Keep the head up and grasp the arms firmly for support. This stunt can also be done from a knee and shoulder balance with top person transferring one arm at a time from the bottom one's knees to his arms.

A good combination is to have both partners lying in a supine position, head to head, grasping each other's arms. The top person executes a back extension up to a low arm-to-arm balance.

11. *Low Low Hand-to-Hand Balance.* The bottom person is in a supine position with the arms along his sides. He bends his arms and raises the hands

upward, keeping his elbows on the mat. The top person stands straddling the bottom one's head and places his hands in the bottom person's hands. The top person then kicks upward into a hand balance on the partner's hands. A spotter should work closely on this stunt. Remember to allow the bottom person to do most of the balancing by shifting his bands and arms. The top one should simply maintain a rigid position.

12. *Low hand-to-hand balance.* The same as the low low hand-to-hand except that the bottom person's arms are raised straight tip from the shoulders, From this position the top person kicks upward into the hand balance position.
13. *High arm-to-arm balance.* The partners stand facing each other with arms raised, and each grasps the other person's upper arm. The top person then leaps towards the bottom one and circles his legs around the bottom person's waist. He swings down between the bottom partner's legs and then back upward toward the high arm-to-arm position. The bottom person swings the top one tip and tries to move under him so that the final part of the stunt can be done with a slight press motion. The top mounter swings freely upward into the high arm-to-arm position allowing the bottom partner to move in and hold him up over his head.
14. *Overhead back arch.* The bottom person places his hand in the small of the top person's back and holds the ankle with his other hand. The top person then jumps upward into an arch position while the bottom person lifts her overhead. Be sure to hold the top person's ankle, as this helps to steady the

balance position. Have one or two spotters to assist while learning this stunt.

15. *Overhead swan.* The bottom person places his bands on the hips of the top person and then the top person jumps upward into the arch balance overhead. Finding the center of position of the top person is very important in maintaining the overhead swan. At first the top person can bold onto the bottom person's arms while overhead, and as balance becomes secure the hands can be released.

Pyramids

Combinations of balancing stunts can be put together to form pyramids. Because of the great number of possible combinations, no attempt will be made to cover specific pyramids. Instead, general principles will be given and the readers can use their own imagination and creativity.

1. The usual shape of pyramids is either a convex curve with the peak in the center or a concave curve with a peak at each end.
2. The performers may be arranged in such formations as a line or a circle and may utilize apparatus or equipment such as parallel bars, vaulting bucks, ladders, chairs, tables, and flags.
3. For large pyramids the group may be arranged in units, each of which could be a pyramid in itself. In this case the highest unit would be in the center, with the lower units at the sides.
4. If the pyramids are being performed as a part of an exhibition, some attempt should be made to select

and arrange the group on the basis of the sizes of the individuals. Ability will be a limiting factor. For example, if a head balance is to be performed on each side of the middle unit, the appearance would be better if two individuals of the same height and build were selected.

5. If the pyramid involves building on top of one another, the stronger and heavier members of the group should be used to form the foundation.
6. Pyramids are usually formed "by the numbers." The group should be lined up in rows with the top people standing behind the bottom people. Then some sort of signal is given for each step or movement until the pyramid is complete, Another signal should be given for the dismount, which usually is done forward and may include a forward roll when the performers hit the mat. The pyramid need not be held for a very long time. The instructor, through watching the performance, can judge the amount of time that would be most effective.
7. Often a lack of ability may be compensated for by having one person held in a balance position by another person. For example, two performers may do hand balances facing each other and have their legs held in place by a third person standing between them. Also, stunts such as merely standing on a kneeling partner's back or on the backs of two people in a push-up position make suitable parts of a pyramid and require no particular ability.

8

RULES AND REGULATIONS

Gymnastics and tumbling comprising some of our most basic motor skills, also include some of the oldest skills. Their beginning is some what obscure, but can be placed at about 2600 B.C., when the Chinese developed a few activities, that resembled gymnastics particularly of the mediaeval type. However, the actual development of gymnastics began in the early Greek and Roman periods of history. The Greeks first gave great emphasis to gymnastics, in fact, the word Gymnastics itself is derived from the Greek. The Spartans were most rigid in providing gymnastic training for their youth and girls as well as boys were expected to be good gymnasts. The early Romans copied the physical training programme from the Greeks but adopted it to their military training programme. With the fall of the Greek and Roman civilizations, gymnastics declined. Perhaps the earliest contributor to the renewed interest was Johann Basedow (1723-1790) of Germany who in 1776 added gymanastic exercises to the programme of instructions in his school. Johann Guts Muths (1759-1839) who is known as the "great grandfather of gymnastics" introduced it into the Prussian schools. He wrote several works on the subject including `Gymnastics for Youth', considered the first book on gymnastics.

Renewed emphasis on gymnastics in World War II Physical training programme resulted in increased growth of that activity in the schools in U.S. after the war. Within the last two decades there has been a phenomenal surge of interest in the sport. Gymnastics in Olympics were first included in the year 1924 in Paris.

Gymnastics

Men

The following Code of points has the purpose of providing an objective and uniform body of rules for exercises in gymnastics at the international level, of promoting the knowledge and abilities of the judges as well as serve the gymnasts and trainer as helpful guidelines for precompetition training and for the formation of exercise. The judges are to adhere to these regulations without any deviation what so ever. In the case of such deviations the judge may be relieved of his duties by the directors responsible for the competition. These regulations should also be used in evaluating national competitions of member federations.

The jury

For meets of the FIG Olympic Games, intercontinental, continental or regional meets or games, the jury for each event consists of five men, namely: one superior judge, and four judges, from the list of international judges, who are nominated any member organizations which take part in the competition. To be selected as an international judge for international, continental or regional games or competitions those in question must fulfil the following prerequisites: The superior judge must be certified by the FIG and must be able to demonstrate to the satisfaction of the TC/FIG, and on the basis of good test results, good knowledge as well as good abilities and indisputable objectivity in judging. The organizers are advised here to add neutral persons. Further, the superior judges to be considered must be entered on the list of internationally certified judges.

The judges nominated by the participating ederations must be entered on the list of nternationally certified judges. Priority should be iven to those who are currently certified and possess valid FIG Brevet. Seating of judges in competitions etween nations and other international competitions f the FIG Technical Regulation, 1982 edition. ccording to these articles the superior judge may not epresent a federation involved in the competition. The umber of neutral judges is based on the agreement nade between the participating federations.

election and announcing of the judges:

- The seeding of judges of the individual nations into judges groups, according to the FIG Technical Regulations, 1982 edition, is the responsibility of the Technical Committee and the technical directors responsible for the conduct of intercontinental, continental and regional games and competitions.
- The results are to be announced to the participating federations immediately.
- The personal nomination of the superior judges is under the control of the TC/FIG and the technical directors of the intercontinental, continental and regional games or meets. Nomination of judges is the responsibility of the participating federations according to the above regulations.

The TCM/FIG reserves the right to unseat judges, who during previously held judges examination were proven incompetent, not objective and violated the rules and regulations.

Recruiting of the jury and representation of the federations:

1. The corps of judges is composed of one or two representatives per participating nation. If the number of judges is insufficient, recruiting will be considered from those federations who in the previous (last) competition of the FIG, or the last Olympic Games, finished among the first ten positions, providing these federations submit nominations. If there are no nominations or too few are present, the jury may be completed by selecting judges from other nations in attendance, as long as such judges fulfil the necessary requirements.
2. For continental or regional games or meets the same practice is to be employed whereby the order of placement in previous competition of an equal level is decisive of the addition of a second judge. If this is not possible from experience or practical reasons, the order of placement of the previous competition of the FIG or that of the last Olympic Games is decisive.
3. For the purpose of completing a numerically insufficient corps of judges an additional nomination is to be requested from each of the ten top federations as well as qualified individual representation.

The additional judges will, in any case, be seated as active judges in one or more of the three competitions, in the Olympic Games, World Championships, Continental or Regional Games or competitions.

4. Should deviations from these regulations arise, under special conditions, the Technical Committee of the FIG makes decisions in all cases, or for other international events, the superior technical authority.

Working procedure of the jury

Tasks and responsibilities of the superior judge:

1. The superior judge is completely responsible for the organisation and the work of the group of judges at his apparatus.
2. He has the task of evaluating objectivity and according to the regulations each exercise, overseeing his four judges and taking part in all phases of judging objectively and according to the regulations.
3. He checks the differences in marks and calls the judge or judges for the purpose of consultation and an eventual change of the mark awarded, when the judging is contrary to the regulations and not objective.
4. He maintains relations with the president of the jury and the directors of competition, the scores, as well as the group leader, and is responsible for the efficient conduct of this event.
5. To signal the start of an exercise—for the group leader, competitors and the jury—he raises a green flag. If special electrical installations are available for the transmission of the scores by the judges, the flag is replaced with a green light. The red light normally signals the end of the competition.

In both cases, i.e., after the green flag has been raised, or the green light has been switched on, the gymnast will raise his right arm in the direction of the superior judge, thus notifying also the judges that he is ready to begin his exercise.

Responsibility and authority of the superior judge and basic score

1. The superior judge is the first to lay his completed score slip on the table, thereby signifying that his mark represents, according to the rules, the exercise without regard to the person or nationality, only the work presented.
2. His mark added to the average of the two middle marks of the four judges, divided by two is the valid basic score. It is used for possible intervention in consultations when needed.
3. If a difference exists between the two middle marks contrary to the rules, the superior judge has the right to make a change toward the basic score. In such a case he calls only the judge or judges involved.
4. Should it happen that all four judges as a result of misinterpretation of the rules, through outside influences, etc. as well as from a technically false interpretation, present scores above or below that of the superior judge and thus above or below the basic score, the superior judge is to call the jury for the purpose of consultation and in a reconciliatory manner attempt to bring about a suitable agreement—decisive here is also the basic score.
5. If a judge repeatedly has scores out of line or if the

favours of disfavours in his marking certain persons or nation, the superior judge is to intervene energetically and to hold the particular judge to objective evaluation. Should after a second such intervention no improvement take place, the superior judge is to report this to the director of the competition who, after further such occurrences on the part of the judge, can exclude the judge or judges involved.

6. In cases of judging which are against rules 3 and 4 or in cases of non-objective actions on the part of a judge where no agreement can be reached, the superior judge is likewise to inform the director of the competition or the president of the jury, who will base his opinion in the first instance on the basic score and the statement of the superior judge. Only then will the judge or judges be heard in order to decide possible differences of opinion meaningfully.
7. Should the director of the competition not be able to bring about a satisfactory agreement, he will consult the jury of appeal 1 whose decision is irrevocable.
8. Consultation on a mark after the first exercise of the day of competition, for the purpose of orientating evaluations, may not take place if the scores are within the framework provided in the regulations.

Duties, rights and tasks of the judges

1. The judges serving at an apparatus are to adhere to all parts of the Code of points, possible written instructions of the TC/FIG, instructions obtained at judges courses and the instructions of the superior

judge, and are completely responsible for the scores the award.

2. They have the duty to attend the judges courses and all scheduled meetings for the competitions for which they have been selected and seeded by the TC/FIG to participate, and are to arrive punctually according to the time and directions in the work plan.
3. Judges who do not take sufficient interest in such meetings, are absent, or appear late for courses and meeting, can be replaced by the director of competition.
4. To perform their duties, judges must possess the Code of points, as well as any special material issued by TC/FIG otherwise they can be replaced by the directors of the competition. The officers of the federations involved assume full responsibility.
5. The judge has the right to file a written protest with the directors of competition in case of arbitrary action taken against him by the superior judge.

Formalities of judging and general remarks

All exercises are scored with points ranging from 0 to 10 with deductions of whole points, half points and 1/10 of a point. The final score is the average of the two middle scores of the four judges. The point difference between the two middle scores my not be greater than:

0.10 with an average of 9.55 and higher
0.20 with an average of 9.00 to 9.50
0.30 with an average of 8.00 to 8.95
0.50 with an average of 6.50 to 7.95

0.80 with an average of 4.00 to 6.45
1.00 in all other cases

Decisive for the average score is the average of the two middle scores. As soon as the difference surpasses the limitation given above, the superior judge is to call a consultation according. This is also to be done in the apparatus finals. The judges' scores will be made public for all competitions following an acoustical or optical signal. Possible corrections of judges scores should be administered by the superior judge before they are made public according to directions given by article 9 of the regulations. The final score depending upon the circumstances will be flashed either simultaneously or following the others. The score of the superior judge is never made public. If within a group of superior judges or judges a language barrier exists which makes necessary conversations impossible, their own federations are to provide and make available suitable translation personnel. This applies to judges' courses, briefing sessions and competitions. It is however, desirable that for world championships and Olympic Games, judges are named who, in addition to their necessary technical knowledge, also possess, as a prerequisite, knowledge of French, German of English. The federations have these responsibilities and are authorised, when necessary, to make arrangements with the organisers.

If a judge or superior judge brings a translator to assist him, the translator's work is limited to translating and he is forbidden to influence the superior judge or judge in any manner. Translators for superior judges are permitted to sit next to them, while translators for judges may not sit next to them but only in their proximity in such a manner that when needed they may be called to their work without loss of time.

Competition attire

Each competitor or each team wishing to take part in competitions of the FIG or Olympic Games or international, continental or regional games or contests must fulfil the following prerequisites for uniform when competing. In competition 1 each team must wear uniform dress of the same colour. Individual gymnasts of one nation, must adhere to this during all competitions as well.

On pommel horse, rings, parallel bars and horizontal bar, all competitors must perform their exercise wearing long white pants with foot wear (socks and gymnastic shoes, or socks only) during all competitions. In floor exercise and vaulting there are two possible alternatives; the competitors my wear long white pants with foot-wear (socks and gymnastic shoes or socks only) or short pants with socks and shoes, socks only or perform bear footed. Wearing of a shirt (jersey) is compulsory during all competitions.

Failure to adhere to points 1-4, will result in a penalty of 0.3 taken from the final score of a gymnast in question.

Spotting or assistance during competitions

For the prevention of accidents and for the moral support of the competitor, only one assistant will be permitted to stand, in the three different competitions, near the following apparatus: horizontal bar, parallel bars, rings and vaulting. Any assistance, contributing to the successful execution of an exercise part or a connection, results in deduction. The deduction for such assistance may range, from 0.5 to 0.7 points depending on the difficulty part. This rule is applied when spotting prevented the gymnast to fall-off the apparatus or execution of an exercise part or connecting part could not have been possible without assistance. If an interruption of an exercise or a fall occurs, despite the assistance, then deductions for execution must be taken in addition to the afforementioned deductions of 0.5-0.7 points for assistance. On the pommel horse and in the floor exercise the presence of a spotter is not permitted. However, if a spotter stands near the apparatus or appears on the podium during the exercise, the gymnast will be penalized 0.3 points. The presence of an additional spotter for the apparatus mentioned in article 13 par.1, in the three competitions, will cause the gymnast, without warning, a deduction of 0.3 points.

If a second spotter appears at the conclusion of an exercise, i.e. when both spotters are on the stage during the exercise, the gymnast will receive a penalty up to 0.2 points, according to the difficulty and/or risk involved in executing the dismount. The regulation in the FIG booklet Apparatus measurements and dimensions provides that all apparatus must be fixed so firmly to the podium that no shaky movements of the apparatus are possible. If an apparatus is held by the team leader or another member of the team while the gymnast is performing there will be a deduction of 0.3 points.

In no case may the team leader or any other official person speak with the gymnast during the performance of his exercise. If this, however, happens, the gymnast will be penalized with a deduction of 0.3 points by the superior judge. Official persons in the above sense are the team leaders, members of a team or members of an individual competition group, the local group leader or other persons who may be within the competition area.

On the horizontal bar and the rings a gymnast may be assisted into the hang position, but he must maintain the correct posture from the moment his feet leave the floor, i.e. the evaluation of the gymnast's exercise begins at the moment he leaves the floor.

Evaluation of optional exercises

The evaluation of optional exercises take place on the basis of three evaluation factors:

(i) Difficulty

(ii) Combination (construction of the exercise)

(iii) Execution.

Under factor 1(i), the judge examines the material value of an exercise; under 1(i), the manner of composition and construction of the exercise and with 1(iii), the correct and technical execution of the selected exercise in regards to content. Optional exercises on the following four apparatus: pommel horse, rings, parallel bars and horizontal bar as well as floor exercise are evaluated in points ranging from 0 to 10.0 points.

Repetition of exercise: None of the optional exercises in principle may be repeated. Repetitions would only be permitted, if a gymnast is forced to interrupt or has to terminate his exercise due to no fault of his own, i.e. through extraordinary circumstances, such as a defect in the apparatus or the platform, or other organizational failures. In such instances, only the superior judge can decide, or when in doubt, the directors of the competition.

The mount on parallel bars: On the parallel bars, for the mount, the use of only one elastic vaulting board is permitted. The vaulting board may be placed on the lower supports of the parallel bars or mats of this height. The use of vaulting board under the parallel bars is permitted. If the gymnast uses more than one vaulting board or it is placed on a higher level, he will be penalized, without prior warning 0.3 points.

Organisational procedures for FIG Competition and Events and format of such events are discussed in related chapters of the 1982 edition of FIG Technical Regulations. The base score for each apparatus is 9.4. According to related articles, the possibility for awarding bonus points is 0.6.

The difficulty and its evaluation

Type of Competition	*D-parts*	*C-parts*	*B-parts*	*A-parts*	*Total*	*Number of parts*
Competition 1	0	2	4	6	4.0	12
Competition 2:						
and 3:	1	3	2	34	4.09	9
Value:	0.8	0.60	0.40	0.2		

To attain the highest possible score for difficulty, the exercises presented during the three competitions on floor, pommel horse, rings, parallel bars and horizontal bar, must contain the above number A-, B-, C-, and D-value parts:

When scoring difficulty, only the difficulty itself, i.e. the actual raw value of an exercise, is to be taken into consideration, which can be evaluated with maximum 4.0 points. If the gymnast, during the three competitions demonstrated all value-parts successfully, he is entitled to receive a maximum 4.0 points for difficulty. When the exercise does not contain the required number of exercise parts, then for the missing value-pars, a global deduction. During competition 2 and 3 each exercise need to be recapitulated by the judges and 12 exercise parts must be demanded.

Evaluation of A-,B-,C- and D-value-parts: If a gymnast demonstrates more than the prescribed number of D- and C-parts, the additional parts can automatically replace the missing A- or B- parts. Contrary to the above, more than the required number of lover value-parts can only partially replace higher value-parts. When this occurs, the correct point differences between the higher and lower difficulty value-parts must be deducted.

Considering the afforementioned facts, evaluation is done by the following principles:

1. Lower difficulty value-parts can always be substituted with higher difficulty value-parts.
2. Higher difficulty value-parts can only partially be substituted with the next lower difficulty value-parts. This does not refer to the A-parts.
3. If the replacement of a higher difficulty level is done only partially, deduction in point value will be the difference between the demonstrated value-part and the next higher difficulty level.

Such decisions should always be in favour of the gymnast.

Awarding scores for difficulty

1. When a D-part is replaced by a C-part only 0.2 points is to be deducted for the missing D-part, this means that a C-part can only partially replace a non executed D-part.
2. If for example in competition 1 B no C-parts, but 6 B- and 6 A-parts are executed- the missing 2 C-parts can only partially be replaced by the extra B-parts. In this case the deduction is 0.4 points, therefore, the maximum total difficulty is only 3.6.
3. If during competition 1 B, an exercise contains only 4 B- and 6 A-parts, the gymnast will loose the total value of the missing 2 C-parts, therefore the deduction will be 1.2 points. The difficulty level of the exercise cannot be higher than 2.8 points.
4. When the gymnast performs only 3 C-and 3 B-parts in competition 1 B, the extra C-part will automatically replace the missing B-part, therefore, the gymnast will not be penalized.

In awarding scores for difficulty, the judge will take into consideration only B-,C- and D-parts - since it can be presumed that in an exercise demonstrating full value for difficulty as well as the necessary number of B-, C-and D-parts, the gymnast demonstrated enough A-parts.

The difficulty component of the total scoring:

1. The difficulty of an exercise must never be escalated at the expense of correct form and technically correct execution. The exercises must therefore, in regards to content be adapted to the

ability of the gymnast. During the exercise construction, the following fundamental principles must be observed: above all, the gymnast is to maintain a complete control over his body. Assurance, elegance and amplitude should constitute the fundamental characteristics of an exercise.

2. Considering these basic principles, described in part 1, a technically correct execution is expected for the recognition of difficulty parts.

Requirements for contents of an exercise in addition to the required difficulty, the following regulations and guidelines must be adhered to:

General combination requirements

1. The parts of an exercise must be connected in an elegant and fluent manner without superfluous movements, intermediate swings, repetitions of parts with the same succeeding or preceding connections, or parts which are too easy with regards to the rest of the exercise.
2. In evaluating the combination it must be considered if the different required D-, C- and B-parts are distributed correctly throughout the entire exercise.
3. The construction of the optional exercise must differ conspicuously from the construction of the compulsory exercise. It should not necessarily be considered as an error if parts or connections from the compulsory exercise are contained in the optional exercise, but in this case the preceding or succeeding connections must be different.

4. The exercise must commence either from a starting position or with a short run. Additional exercise parts are not allowed between the run and the mount.
5. Dismounts from the apparatus and at the end of the floor exercise routine must be completed in a stand with feet together. Pushing off from the apparatus with the feet to perform a dismount is not permitted.

Evaluation of the combination

1. If the construction of an exercise does not meet the requirements, a deduction made for each violation is 0.3
2. For every intermediate swing, the deduction will be...... 0.3
3. If the dismount is not commensurate with the difficulty of the rest of the exercise, the deduction is .... up to 0.3
4. If an exercise is not finished with a real dismount or if the dismount is only partially executed, the deduction is.. 0.3 to 0.5
5. If from the exercise the required C-part or B-part is missing, the deduction is 0.3
6. If D-, C- and B-parts are not built to serve the purpose of the exercise, the deduction is.. up to 0.2
7. For each connecting part or part of no value that does not correspond to the general difficulty level of the exercise, the deduction is 0.2

8. If part of an exercise is repeated several times even though the connections before and after may be different, the deduction is 0.2
9. If the combination of an exercise resembles the compulsory exercise too strongly, the deduction is .... up to 0.5
10. If the optional exercise ends with the compulsory dismount with the same preceding connection, the deduction is 0.3
11. If the optional exercise is performed exactly the same as the compulsory exercise, the gymnast will receive zero score (0.0 points)
12. If the exercise does not contain 12 required parts described in Article 22, the deduction for deficiency in combination is 0.2
13. If the gymnast dismounts by pushing off from the apparatus with his feet, the deduction is 0.5

Floor exercise

a) If the gymnast before his tumbling passes performs more than 3 steps the deduction is 0.3

b) If the exercise is too short or too long in time duration the deduction is:

up to 2 seconds 0.1

up to 5 seconds 0.2

up to 9 seconds 0.3

more than 9 seconds 0.5

c) If the gymnast leaves the floor exercise area, the deduction each time is 0.1

d) The floor exercise area is 12 x 12m. All parts of this area must be fully used, without stepping out of the area.

e) Using a special watch, deductions for deficiency and excessive use of time is made by line judge 1. Deductions for stepping out of the area is indicated to respectively assigned line judge.

Pommel Horse

a) If one part of the horse is not used, the deduction is 0.3

b) If the exercise is done only on the pommels, the deduction is 0.6

c) If the distribution of the exercise on the three parts of the horse tends to be very one sided, the deduction is 0.2

d) If the exercise contains only one scissor, the deduction is 0.3

e) If the exercise contains no scissor at all, deduction is 0.6

f) If the gymnast favours certain exercise parts during the performance of his exercise, the deduction is .... 0.3 to 0.5

Rings

a) Based on special requirements stated under point 1, for each missing strength part, the deduction is 0.3

b) If the meaningful distribution of swinging parts, strength and hold parts does not correspond to the requirements, the deduction is 0.2

c) If there is no handstand executed with swing, the deduction is 0.3

Parallel Bars

a) If at least one B-part in the exercise is not executed with a simultaneous grip release, the deduction is 0.3

b) If more than 3 pronounced hold parts are performed, the deduction is, each time 0.1

c) When the exercise does not contain a swing C-part, in all three optional exercise competition the deduction is 0.3

Horizontal Bar

a) For all hold or strength parts, the deduction each time is 0.2

b) If any of the special requirements are missing 0.3

For poor form and incorrect technical execution deductions will have to be made.

1. Execution errors in form apply to: Insufficient toe point, incorrect leg, head, arm, and body positions.
2. The following examples of incorrect technical execution are:

   — Insufficient swing, lack of amplitude and harmony among various exercise parts.

— If the gymnast cannot perform an exercise part of its correct end position for example: to handstand.

— When the gymnast during free support scales or hanging scales cannot maintain a completely horizontal body, or his arms are horizontal holding the cross.

Deductions for technical insufficiency of the execution

1. Walking in handstand: 0.1 per step, maximum deduction 0.5
2. Interrupted motion in upward movements, the deduction is 0.3
3. Two or more attempts to perform a hold or a strength part or to any other special upward movement, the deduction is .... 0.2 to 0.5
4. Strength parts that are executed with swing parts that are executed with strength shall be penalized with .... up to 0.3
5. Support scales, hanging scales and L-positions are not held in horizontal position or the elbows are bent, the deductions is: .... up to 0.3
6. The time duration for hold parts is 2 seconds. When the required 2 seconds hold is not honoured, the deductions are as follows:

a) Holding for 1 second only, the deduction is 0.2

b) If an exercise part is not held at all: When this occurs, the exercise in question does not contain hold parts and there may be combination deductions. This can also be regarded as deficiency in hold parts and as a consequence, the difficulty part may not be given its full value.

7. If an exercise is not completed with a good stand or it during the exercise incorrect posture or similar faults are made, the deductions are the following:
   a) Small step or hop, or incorrect posture after an exercise the deduction is .... up to 0.2
   b) several steps or hops or touching the floor with one or two hands without support, or bad posture after the exercise, the deduction is .... up to 0.3
   c) Support with one or two hands on the floor, kneel, to seat or other falls.. 0.3-0.5

8. If an exercise part or connecting part lacking harmony, rhythm, flexibility and amplitude, the deduction in each case is 0.2 If the afforementioned faults are prevalent throughout the entire exercise, the deduction is .... up to 1.0

9. When gymnastic movements and connections are not executed according to correct technique, the deduction is ... up to 0.3

10. If during the free standing scales the legs are not straight or the arms or legs are not properly aligned with the trunk the deduction is .... up to 0.2
11. Interruption of an exercise without falling off, the deduction is .... up to 0.3
12. Falling or sitting on the apparatus, the deduction is .... 0.3 to 0.2
13. If during the execution of a salto the legs are apart, the deduction is .... up to 0.2
14. If the landing is done with legs apart, the deduction is .... up to 0.2
15. Handstand executed with bent arms, the deduction is .... 0.2 to 0.3
16. Swinging of ropes, the deduction i .... up to 0.3
17. Unplanned fall from handstand, the deduction is .... up to 0.5
18. If during the felge type movements or movements executed in support the arms are excessively bent, the deduction is .... up to 0.3
19. Forward scissors, without hip movements, which means that the horizontal line does not pass through the upper hip and the shoulder of the supporting arm; or backward scissors, where the upper hip is not at least half way between, the supporting shoulder and horse-body results in deduction each time of .... up to 0.2

Touching the apparatus

Touching the body of the horse, the pommels, the rails, the standards for the parallel bars, the floor, or the base support of the parallel bars; the horizontal bar, the uprights of the horizontal bar; or the ropes of the rings. Touching these with the feet, legs or with the seat or other parts of the body if the touching of these is not required by the nature of the movements, every time the deduction is .... up to 0.3

Interruption of an exercise through falling, loosing the grip, or without loosing the grip with weight on the floor

1. When falling from the apparatus or standing on the floor without releasing the grip and interrupting the exercise, the exercise part may not be repeated, but continued immediately or at the latest within 30 seconds. The deduction for the fall will be 0.5
2. If the exercise is not continued at the end of these 30 seconds, it shall be considered completed, and the value of the exercise in this case will be limited to the work done up to the interruption.
3. The superior judge checks the time and informs the gymnast at the completion of 10,20 and 30 seconds. He then calls <<time>> at the end of the 30 seconds.
4. When continuing the exercise, the gymnast

must not repeat the last completed part of the exercise, but must start with the part that follows. Movements that are needed here in order to arrive at the proper starting position shall not be considered in the evaluation of the exercise, unless the gymnast uses more than one intermediate or preparatory swings or attempts to arrive in the starting position.

5. When the exercise is interrupted due to tearing of clothing or hand grips, loosening of bandages or any other health problems, the above rules will prevail.

Application of bonus points

Since the base score in all three competitions is 9.4 a total of 0.6 bonus points may be given.

1. Awarding bonus points will be done in the following manner:
   a) For courage in difficulty and/or combination Bonus points for courage cannot be awarded unless D-parts or D- combinations are presented .... up to 0.2
   b) For originality in combination and/or difficulty .... up to 0.2
   c) For virtuosity in execution.............. up to 0.2
2. In exceptional cases, an additional 0.1 point may be awarded for either courage or

originality, provided the 0.2 points in either category have not been exhausted and the exercise contains additional parts shown by the gymnast, which are performed with either courage or excellent original technique. points for courage cannot be awarded unless D-parts or D-combinations are presented Evaluation of technical execution is the following:

In case of good technical execution .... up to 0.2

Faulty technical execution 0.1

In case of a fall or support 0.0

3. Awarding bonus points totalling 0.6 points for one part is not permitted.

The maximum bonus points awarded for one element is 0.4

Discipline and behaviour during competitions

For undisciplinary and unsportsmanlike behaviour in all cases during the framework of a competition or manifestation is penalized 0.3 points.

Unsportsmanlike and undisciplined behaviour is: Breaking rules and incorrect behaviour. For example:

— Delaying the start of an exercise after green signal has been flashed.

— Wearing the incorrect competitive number.

— Team leaves the competition area without permission.

— Coach is standing near apparatus during the execution of an exercise during the competition.

The gymnast has no right to leave the competition area without written permission from the official doctor of the competition. Violation of this rule will result in exclusion from the competition.

The evaluation of compulsory exercises

1. The evaluation of compulsory exercises is based on the following factors:
   a) The exercise presented must be identical with the prescribed text. Maximum base score is 9.8.
   b) The exercise must be presented flawlessly, free of technical or general execution errors.
2. With factor 1.a) above, the judge determines if the exercise is being executed according to the prescribed text, while with factor 1.b) above, he evaluates the form and technical aspects of the execution of the exercise.
3. In order to enable correct evaluation, every compulsory exercise is divided into different parts, which indicate a certain value in points corresponding to the difficulty rating of the various parts.
4. Apart from the necessary A-parts, every compulsory exercise also contains 4 to 5 B-parts. The exercise, in relation to the optional exercises on the particular apparatus, has a content value of 9.8 i.e. when the exercise is executed according to the prescribed text.
5. The missing 0.2 points bringing the score to a total of 10 points may be obtained from the bonus points for special virtuosity.

The compulsory exercises including the vault, may in principle not be repeated. Repetitions are allowed as even stipulated for optional exercises, only when the gymnast through no fault of his, has to interrupt or terminate his exercise due to exceptional circumstances, such as defects in the apparatus or other unforeseen deficiencies in organisation. Decisions on such repeats can only be made by the superior judge of when in doubt, the directors of the competition.

Deductions for errors in the interpretation of compulsory exercises: If the exercises are not executed according to the prescribed text, the deductions are as follows:

1. For parts or connecting parts that are omitted, deduct the entire value of the particular part as provided. In making these deductions, it is necessary to determine whether the omission of a particular part or connecting parts make the previous or following parts easier. If this is the case, deduct an additional 0.1 to 0.3 points.
2. For added parts, the deduction everytime is 0.3 points. It is necessary here, also, to determine if the addition of this part made the previous or the following parts easier. If this is the case, deduct an additional 0.1 to 0.3 points.
3. If a definite part or a definite connecting part of the compulsory exercise is to be performed on one particular side, but is performed by the gymnast on the wrong side, he loses one-half of the allotted value of the part or connecting part.

Evaluation of execution of compulsory exercises: In grading the execution and technical aspects of a compulsory exercise use the same standards as for the optional exercises, including intermediates swings, interruptions of exercises, etc. Exception can only be made when the Technical Committee releases special rules for the compulsory exercises.

Evaluation in the finals

1. The evaluation in finals, for the title in the individual AA competition (6-event-competition with optional exercises, i.e. in regional games) and for the titles for each event are made by principle according to the regulations for evaluation in competition 1.

2. Exercises during finals can have the same form as in Competition 1 B and Competition 2 but they must meet all difficulty requirements stated.

3. In Competition 2, the finals for the individual AA will, according to FIG/TR, the 36 best gymnasts from Competition 1 be admitted, thus about 1/3 of all participants, which is also valid for regional games.

4. In Competition 3 for the finals in each event, participation, according to FIG/TR is by the 8 best gymnasts determined by the addition of compulsories plus the optionals on each apparatus in Competition 1. If one or several gymnasts qualifying for the finals decline, according to the applicable article of the Technical Regulations to participate in one or more apparatus, the next following gymnasts will be considered for the finals. The applies for the Olympic Games as well.

5. The directors of the meet will name, for Competition 2 and 3, besides the finalists, 2 additional gymnasts, the 2 next in order as alternates.

These gymnasts must be prepared to compete until the start of the first event of Competition 2 and the respective event during Competition 3, until the first gymnast begins the Competition.

Additional rules for evaluating exercises in the finals

1. Concerning application of bonus points.
2. If the gymnast remains within the usual adequate limits of the three evaluation factors, he cannot receive more than 9.4 points for his performance. If he exceeds these limits in one, two or even three of these evaluation factors, he is then entitled to the bonus point factors a), b) and c). The 3 components of bonus points in reference to difficulty and/or combination are courage and/or originality. Virtuosity is mentioned only in relation with execution.
3. The judge has to determine how to apply awarding courage, originality and virtuosity successfully, based on points a), b), c).
4. Furthermore, the judge has to observe and determine if courage, originality and/or virtuosity limits itself to one or two parts, if they influence half of the exercise, or if the entire exercise is equally influenced by one, two or even all of the bonus point factors.
5. Under no circumstances can the gymnast receive bonus points on the basis of merely increasing the

difficulty, if the increased difficulty shows no real courage or real originality.

6. According to courage may be awarded only if a D-part is demonstrated. Competition 1 B, does not require a D-part, therefore in order for the gymnast to receive bonus point for courage, he must execute at least one D-part.
7. The judge will find useful definitions of terms courage, originality and virtuosity and he must abide by these definitions and additional supplements issued by the Technical Committee in all respects.
8. After rewarding bonus points, the total score may never exceed 10.0 points.
9. The following examples represent a picture of the bonus point possibilities as well as their influence on the final score and tell you at the same time how to fill in your score sheets.

Competitions 1,2 and 3 Examples	1	2	3	4	5	6	7	8
Maximum Score	9.4	9.4	9.4	9.4	9.4	9.4	9.4	9.4
—Deductions	0.5	0.4	0.5	0.4	0.2	0.1	0.1	0.1
Base Score	8.9	9.0	8.9	9.0	9.2	9.3	9.3	9.3
+Courage	0.0	0.1	0.1	0.0	0.3	0.1	0.3	0.2
+Originality	0.0	0.0	0.1	0.3	0.0	0.3	0.0	0.2
+Virtuosity	0.2	0.1	0.1	0.1	0.0	0.0	0.2	0.2
Final Score	9.1	9.2	9.2	9.4	9.5	9.7	9.8	9.9

The composition of the jury in the finals

1. For Competition 2 the composition of the jury is based on the respective article in the FIG Technical Regulation, 1982 edition.
2. For Competition 3 the jury must be composed in each event as follows:
   a) Two superior judges and four judges of which one head-judge and four judges must come from nations not participating in this event.
   b) The superior judge is the chief of the jury for the event. He consults the second superior judge, calls the judges for a discussion on the scores and he gives the score sheet to the scoring personnel.
   c) If no common understanding can be found after consultation, the score to be given by the superior judges will be the average of their individual scores.

Vaulting

General

1. All vaults must begin with the run and executed with support of one or both hands, over the horse placed longways, without support zones. The length of running approach is optional, however, it must not be longer than 25 metres, counted from the vertical line of the near horse-end.
2. Compulsory and optional vaults may be executed only once each; and the compulsory vault may not be repeated in any of the 3 competitions as optional vault.

3. For Competition 3, where 2 different vaults with one trial for each must be executed, these must be performed one after another.
4. The evaluation starts when the gymnast begins the run, the latter is not taken into consideration for evaluation; and finishes after the landing, with feet together, in a perfect stand.
5. A support zone may be set for the compulsory vault, but it must be listed in the table of Evaluation for compulsory exercises, issued by TC/FIG.

The evaluation of the horse vault is divided into five (5) individual factors:

1. Base score, according to Article 55 or description of the compulsory vault.
2. Preflight, up to the moment the hands leave the horse.
3. Second flight phase (post-flight), after hands leave horse up to and including the stand.
4. Execution during the vault.
5. Awarding of possible bonus points for originality and/or virtuosity. These factors are to be considered by the judges as follows:
    a) Factor 1 can be found in Difficulty Table in the Code of Points, therefore it is simply a material matter.
    b) Factor 2 and 3 must be evaluated from a technical point of view.

c) Factor 4 refers to execution in relation to form, and factor 5 refers to awarding possible bonus points.

The level of difficulty and form of various vaults

1. The drawing in illustrates the difficulty levels and forms of the different vaults in the 3 competitions. Contrary to evaluation on the apparatus, a vault cannot be devalued due to faulty technical execution, unless the vault is so badly done that its original character has changed completely.
2. The vaults known up to now appear in 4 degrees of difficulty and accompanied with their base score.

   In regard to this information the judge can see the score of difficulty to be considered as the base score.
3. Vaults not listed in these articles can be evaluated by a comparison with listed existing vaults in order to find the difficulty level.
4. In order to encourage the gymnasts to demonstrate original vaults, according to all 3 competitions bonus points must be considered.
5. The vaults executed with support on one hand have a higher value in regard to those executed with the support on two hands.

The pre-flight and the initial front support on the horse in view of execution must meet the prescribed technical requirements as specified for a given vault.

The role of the initial front support is to create an optimum condition to execute the post-flight and as a result the post-flight will be executed higher. The pre-flight begins with a take-off from vaulting board and ends at the moment of support on one or two hands. In order to evaluate a given vault correctly, the judge must take the following basic characteristics of the pre-flight into consideration:

1. Adequate speed, which makes a smooth transition possible to arrive in front support without interruption in rhythm.
2. Besides the adequate stretch of the body combined with correct posture, the legs must be straight and together at the moment the gymnast leave the vaulting board. Deductions for faulty execution may be found.

The second phase is the last part of the vault. The initiate the post-flight, the gymnast must push off from the horse vigorously in order to attain a flight pattern which shows maximum height and distance.

The post-flight begins with a push from the horse and ends with the landing. In order to obtain the maximum score for technical execution the judge must take the following rules in to consideration.

1. The body must rise in such a way, that the buttocks reach the height of at least 1 metre above the horse. This is the major characteristics of a well executed vault. If this height of the body and buttocks are not attained at the right moment, there should be an appropriate deduction.
2. In the same line of thoughts as in the first paragraph of Article 48 the power of amplitude and flight must bring the body in horizontal distance

and in a standing position on the floor which, measured from the end of the horse, must be 2 metres. Again here the buttocks, in good body position, characteristics of various vaults, play an important role. If this distance is not attained in good body position, there will be appropriate deductions.

3. The drawing below gives a better explanation of 1 and 2.
4. In the technical execution of a vault the direction of the flight is very important. It must follow the line of the length of the horse, if not, it will bring appropriate deductions.

For practical reasons, the following paragraphs include all possible deductions, except difficulty:

1. The difficulty score is obtained from the applicable instructions in the Code of points for optional vaults and the interpretation of the compulsory vault.
2. For errors during pre-flight, including the support on one or two hands, according to applicable rules, and in the minimum requirements are not fulfilled, the deduction is .... up to 1.5
3. If during the post-flight counting from the horizontal body position the height does not reach the required 1 meter but only 0.5 metre and the distance from the horse to the landing does not reach the required 2 metres but only 1 metre the

deduction for both cases is 0.5 altogether 1.0. The deduction may be increased if the vault does not satisfy these requirements up to 0.5

4. If during the vault and upon landing, the gymnast does not assume a position in the direction of the longitudinal axis of the horse, the deductions are as follows:
   a) during the flight .... up to 0.3
   b) at arrival to stand .... up to 0.2
   c) for a) and b) together .... up to 0.5
5. If the gymnast takes a run more than 25 metres, the deduction is 0.3
6. Too pronounced bending of the body forward or backward in hecht vaults, handsprings etc. provided such bending is not required for the type of vaults .... up to 0.5
7. Poor position of feet, arms, legs, head or body or parting the legs when the vautt does not require it, each time .... up to 1.0
8. Bent arms in handsprings, yamashitas and hecht vaults, the deduction is .... 0.3 to 0.5
9. Deductions for errors in stand after the vault: The stand after the vault is to be judged in the same manner as a stand after an exercise on the apparatus:
   a) Small step or hop, or otherwise poor form, the deduction is .... up to 0.2

b) Several steps or hops as in a) or touching the floor with hands, or one hand without support on floor, or poor form, the deduction is............ up to 0.3

c) Support with both hands or hand on floor, kneeling, sitting or other falls, the deduction is .... 0.3 to 0.5

10. Concerning possibilities for bonus points.

11. A vault will receive a zero score for the following:

  a) If the gymnast completes the run, but runs past the horse, i.e. completed an attempt.

  b) If the gymnast starts running and stops, runs back and takes a second start to complete the vault.

  c) When the vault was so poorly executed, that it cannot be recognized or he is pushing off with his feet form the horse.

  d) If the gymnast double touches the horse.

  e) If on landing, the feet do not hit the ground before any other body part.

  f) If in competition 1 B, 2 and 3, the compulsory vault is performed as an optional.

Seating arrangements of judges for vaulting

1. The four judges and the superior judge shall be

seated in such a way that they can, from each position, see every vault without obstruction.

2. Seating of the superior judge and the four judges can be arranged in a straight line, but in this case, the distance between them cannot be less than 1 metre.

3. When the apparatus are mounted on a platform according to the Technical Regulations, the organizers shall make certain that chairs of the superior judge and judges are placed in adequate height in order that they may, at a glance, observe the area in a horizontal plane between the floor and the top of the horse.

Remarks pertaining the vaults:

1. The values of all vaults from A, B, C and D are to be found next to the number in question. From this base score, deductions are to be made for errors of general and technical nature. Bonus points may be awarded for virtuosity up to 0.2 points for all listed vaults.

2. Simple vaults must be evaluated as follows:

Base score 7.0

— Squat vault

Base score 8.0

— Straddle vault with 1/2 turn

— stoop vault with 1/2 turn

— simple Hollander

Awarding possible bonus points in all three competitions:

1. The vaults shown according to their difficulty, are categorised into A-, B-, C-and D-value groups with the following base score.

   A = 9.0, B = 9.2, C = 9.4, D = 9.6.

2. Additional bonus points up to 0.2 may be awarded for virtuosity for vaults in A-, B-, C-and D-categories. Bonus points for courage are already included in the base score.
3. For new vaults shown in the C-and D-categories, bonus points may be awarded up to 0.2 for originality.
4. Awarding bonus points up to 0.3 for courage and originality explained does not apply for vaulting.
5. Errors for general and technical execution according to chapter must be deducted from the base score.

Table of information for awarding bonus points according

Value categories	*A*	*B*	*C*	*D*
Basic score	9.0	9.2	9.4	9.6
Courage	Already included in the base score			
Originality	no	no for new and rare vaults		
Virtuosity	yes	yes	yes	yes
Maximum points 10.0	9.2	9.4	9.8	

Regulations for execution of vaulting in all three competitions

1. In team competition and All Around Competition, only one vault with one attempt is permitted, while

in Competition 3 two different vaults must be presented. Vaults used in these competitions cannot be the same as the compulsory vault, but vaults demonstrated in competition 1 B may be used in Competition 2 and 3 or vice versa.

2. For the two different vaults, the gymnast is allowed only one attempt for each.
3. For showing the same vault twice, a penalty of 0.4 points is given. This deduction is taken from the total points awarded for the second vault.
4. If the compulsory vault is used as one of the two vaults, the gymnast will receive 0.0 points. The two vaults must immediately follow one after the other.
5. In Competition 1 B and 2 as well, the compulsory vault may not be used.

Method of scoring in the three competitions

1. For Competition 1, the scores of the compulsory and optional vaults are added- a maximum of 20 points.
2. For Competition 2, the optional vault produces a maximum of 10 points, to which is added one half of the total score obtained in Competition 1. This may produce a maximum total possible of 20 points.
3. For Competition 3, the procedure is as follows: 1st vault: Maximum 10 points + 2nd vault: maximum 10 points = 20 possible points: 2 = 10 possible points. These possible 10 points are added to one half of the 20 possible points in vaulting, obtained in Competition 1, which produce an over all total of 20 possible points.

Abbreviations of gymnastic nomenclature: To shorten the extent of A-, B-, C- and D-tables, the following abbreviations of gymnastic nomenclature may be used:

b.......................... both L.............................. leg, legs

b.L......................both legs

I..left

bnt...........................bent <L>> supt..<<L>> support

cr.gr...................cross grip mg.......................mixed grip

d.L..................double legs obl.........................obliquely

El.gr.........................Elgrip ogr......ordinary or over grip

f................,............from

p...........................pommel(s)

fr.c......................free circle r.................................. right

frtws...................frontways rgr......................reverse grip

f.s.....................from stand rwa.........................rearways

fwd....................forward sdws..gymnastic) 1144 SB

Conventional (Commonly used) terms: Under conventional terms we describe different exercise parts and connections which received their names after a gymnast who demonstrated, for the first time, these parts at important international competitions and in addition, the FIG Technical Committee recognized them as bonafide exercise parts, this is one way to express gratitude to these gymnasts, who by creating new elements contributed, to a large extend, to the developmental level of artistic gymnastics. Furthermore, with the help of these conventional terms elimination of complicated terminology became possible. During the past few years, proliferations of these conventional terms became evident.

Exercise parts and combinations with prescribed technical execution

In the tables covering exercises of graded difficulty there are also certain B-and C-and D-parts included, which, to be counted as such, are required to be performed in a certain technical way. Where this is the case, the necessary details follow the description such as: <<2 seconds>>, <<in an angle of at least 45 degrees>>, <<body horizontal and arms stretched>>, etc. If such parts or combinations are not performed according to the regulations, they not only lose their B, C- or D-value, but also there may be some deduction for unsatisfactory technical execution in certain cases. If a gymnast, however, has shown the required number of B-, C-or D-parts and if his performance contains additional parts or combinations according to 1, than these additional elements do not have to display the above requirements, therefore they are not to be counted as faults. However, deductions for errors committed of general or technical nature must be made.

Here mainly strength and hold parts or connections are involved, which are not shown for the prescribed time or not held at all, salto backwards on parallel bars without holding, or cross without holding for 2 seconds, but as far as movement and combination is concerned, well performed. Duration of hold parts, execution of strength and swing parts: Execution of strength and hold parts, described according to given material and special requirements may be evaluated by the following:

a) Rhythm must be even until the final position is reached,

b) The entire time duration must be observed and counting of 2 sec must not commence until the final position is established.

In all cases, where strength parts are indicated or where <<slow>> or <<raise>> is mentioned, the gymnast i required to execute these parts slowly and with strength (exception: the arm movements in the floor exercise), i.e., swing must not be applied. If the gymnast shows more than the required number of strength parts, the part must be performed with correct technical execution. However, all technical execution errors must be penalized with the exception of time duration which does not have to be observed. In case of swing parts, the opposite must apply:

- Swing parts have to be executed in a swinging way without the use of strength.
- There should not be an interruption in rhythm and according to the above until the final position is reached, swing must predominate.

Pommel horse and horizontal bar exercises may not contain strength and hold parts under any circumstances. On the above apparatus when the application of strength causes a complete stop. Supports or hangs with straddled legs are classified as a lower value with regard to an execution with legs closed together.

Repetitions of parts or connecting parts: Since repetition of certain exercise parts and connections are unavoidable, the rule makes it possible that they may be repeated only once. For example: Stutzkehre on parallel bars or felge on rings, etc. In those cases where the number of allowable repetitions is exceeded, the judge must determine if the deduction is for repetition of difficulty parts or an error in combination. The above is decided by the following basic principles:

a) Difficulty factor:

<<During the exercise, a value part is allowed to be given credit only twice>>.

b) Combination factor:

<<A value part is allowed to be repeated only once>>.

If a difficulty part is repeated, then it can be recognized only once again as part of the difficulty requirement. Certain connecting parts are the exception to this rule, for example: back handsprings on floor, felges on rings, double leg circles on pommel horse, giant swings on horizontal bar and additional exercise parts which the gymnast performs twice in succession without connecting parts to achieve an ultimate effect. For example: front salto immediate front salto, backward salto immediate backward salto on parallel bars and two consecutive

Definitions and analyses of A-, B-, C- and D-value-parts: According to Article 21, the optional exercises have to consist of a certain number of parts and combinations to gain the highest score given for difficulty. They are divided into 4 different levels of difficulty and called A,B-,C-and D-parts. These tables serve the judge, technician and gymnast as a reference-guide. This arrangement, into groups of different values, requires the judge to be able to discern, and when other parts and connecting parts which are not listed in the tables, can be given credit. His knowledge of gymnastics and his intuition combined with the following tables, explanations, analysis, and evaluations will assist him in judging exercises. Exercise parts and connections are divided into different groups according to their origin and construction. In these groups, A-parts represent the easiest value parts. The value of the difficulty level increases on the horizontal direction through the B- and C-parts up to the D-parts. This is called the definition of the value parts on the horizontal direction.

The concepts of courage, originality and virtuosity

During the development of artistic gymnastic the role of bonus points became more and more evident. These changes placed additional responsibility on the judges. According to the Code of points, the judge has the possibility to award bonus point for the gymnast, particularly those who perform their exercises from the contents point of view above average, showing special courage, virtuosity and originality. The judge must take into consideration, whether or not the contents of the exercise, its technical style made a significant contribution for the development of artistic gymnastics. Since decisions in these matters are not an easy task, passing judgement must not be taken lightly. Bonus points for each category must be evaluated separately, even if the exercise contains courage, virtuosity and originality together.

In an exercise courage factor is present when parts, connections and perhaps the entire exercise is presented in such a way, that the danger of failure at any given moment is present and the gymnast requires all his courage to present an above average performance. When the gymnast is not prepared to perform his task with courage, because he is not skilled in the area of technique and therefore this becomes an obstacle, in a true sense of the word, courage can not be considered. In this case Code of points is violated, which states that the difficulty of an exercise must never be increased at the cost of proper form and technically correct execution. In gymnastic, courage, in all cases must go hand in hand with perfect execution. Bonus points must not be awarded carelessly, on the contrary, in certain instances penalties must be applied.

Women

Purpose

The following Code of points has the task:

- to guarantee the most objective and uniform judgment of exercises in artistic gymnastics at the international level
- to advance the knowledge and skill of the judges and
- to serve as helpful orientation for the gymnasts as well as coaches in the construction of exercises and the preparation for competitions.

The Code is based on the Technical Regulations (TR) as well as he fundamental decisions of the FIG authorities. They take into consideration extensively the modern development of artistic gymnastics in all the world. The Head Judges and judges are obliged to hold themselves to this Code without subjective interpretation, otherwise, they can be dismissed from their positions by the competition leaders. The Technical Committee of FIG recommends that the member federations of FIG also apply this Code of Points for evaluation of national competitions and international contests. The judgement of compulsory and optional exercises at FIG Competitions takes place in Competition 1a, ib and II by

- 1 Head Judge - 6 Judges and - 1 Scientific Technical Collaborator (STC):

  in Competition III by

- 2 Head Judges - 6 Judges and - 1 STC

are able to be place-inserted.

The STC may be from the organizing country. For the formation of the judging panel, the prescriptions of the TR, Edition 1982, 16-5 and 16-6 are to be adhered to. The Head Judge, STC, and Assistant sit at an angle of 90 degree from the middle of the apparatus in a distance which allows a correct and undisturbed observation of the exercise. The Determination of the Average Score: The six scores of the judges are used for the evaluation. The highest and lowest scores are eliminated; the four middle scores are added and divided by four = Average Score.

Rights and Duties of the President of the FIG/WTC

- She conducts that intercontinental Course for the judges.
- She is responsible for the judges' Course before the Competitions (OG,WC, and World Cup).
- She appoints lecturers for continental, international and national judges courses.
- She is responsible for the special course for the Scientific Technical Collaborators (STC).
- She is responsible for the draw of Head Judges,

whose places are filled by members of the FIG/ WTC at the OG, WC, and World Cup.

- She conducts the draw of Judges for use in the competition (OG, WC and World Cup).
- She has the right to consult with the Head Judge, if in her opinion the Average Scores are too high or too low in comparison to the scores on the other apparatus (same standard for all apparatus).
- She takes the deductions for incorrect competition attire:
- In Competition I and II from the All Around total,
- In Competition III from the Average Score of the respective apparatus.
- She conducts the Protest Meeting with the Jury.
- After a change of score, she corrects the official score sheets and signs them.
- In collaboration with the FIG/WTC and the Jury of Appeal she is able to:
- remove Head Judges or judges from the competition, if insufficient expert knowledge or subjective evaluation activity is able to be proven (work with red and yellow cards);
- expel Trainers (male and female) from the podium, if they violate the Regulations by their behaviour.
- She handles all technical organizational matters of the competition with the Members of the FIG/WTC and effects the checking over of the:
- apparatus according to the Norms of the FIG;

- signals, timing devices, score sheets, etc.
- She gives the Organizing Committee corresponding information concerning all questions that pertain to the competition.

Rights and Duties of the Coach

- She must know the Code of points and behave according to the rules.
- She may be on the podium during the competition only to remove the board at the bars and the beam, but may not obstruct the view of the judges.
- During the competition she may not have contact with other persons with the exception of the team doctor, delegation leader and pianist and, if necessary, with the Head Judge jointly with the President of FIG/WTC.
- She may not give signs or audible incitement to action to the gymnast during the exercise and may not touch the apparatus (deduction each time 0.20 Pt.).
- Questions concerning the evaluation (scoring) by her are not allowed.
- Submission of protests.

Trainers (male and female) are to stay with the team in the inner arena circle during the competition (maximum 2 persons).

Compulsory and Optional Exercises

In principle, the compulsory and optional exercises may not be repeated. Exceptions: Defects in the apparatus, lack of organization, or similar things that occur through no fault of the gymnast.

The repetition of an exercise can only occur by decision of the Head Judge of the respective apparatus; in dubious cases, the Jury. When Competitions Ia and Ib are performed, the optional exercises must be different from the compulsory exercises.

Elements from the compulsory exercise may be executed in the optional exercise, but with other connections before and after the element. Maximally, an original compulsory connection of three elements may be executed in the optional. If a gymnast shows more than 3 compulsory elements in an original compulsory connection, the compulsory mount or compulsory dismount in the optional exercise, then a deduction of 0.30 each time occurs. Only the compulsory and optional exercise on the balance beam and floor are subject to a prescribed time limit. The Assistants begin timing when the gymnast takes off from the springboard, mat, or floor or begins on floor with the first movement of her exercise.

INDEX